To: margaret

The Sheila Anthony-Shaw Story

A Memoir

Sheila Anthony-Shaw

Sheila Anthony-Shaw

With closing contribution from Bryan Shaw

Table of Contents

Foreword

What drove a woman to keep searching for answers after more than fifty-five misdiagnoses by more than fifty-five doctors and specialists?

You will find the answer before you read the first chapter of this book; but you'll be compelled to keep reading as you become more and more fascinated by the events of Sheila Anthony-Shaw's extraordinary life.

Her memoir is enjoyable and sheds light on her abilities, determination, and accomplishments. Each piqued while she was enduring psychological and physical duress.

If you were there at the time, you'd never know it. That's because Sheila is uncompromisingly determined to make the best of every moment. How she does this is amazing.

Her resilience is our gift; but so is her (previously) untold story. At the end of the book, her husband, Bryan shares his perspective with a candid contribution.

He talks about how he fell in love with Sheila; but he also addresses the practices, procedures, and effectiveness of America's healthcare system. Finally, he expresses gratitude for miracle worker, Dr. David C. Wright.

I had the privilege of coaching Sheila through the literary

process. I'm pretty sure she had no idea what she was signing up for—not that it mattered.

Sheila's up for—and typically masters—any challenge that comes her way. That's why it's not surprising that her charisma, inexhaustible vitality, and optimism are among her most striking hallmarks.

She's always up for adventure; and where there is no adventure, she's going to create one.

As you read her memoir you'll be moved by her struggles, victories, and most importantly, her resiliency. You'll be moved to recalibrate what you believe is possible for your own life.

This is a story of healing and hope. It illustrates that we all have the ability to do just about anything.

Holding tightly to the principles of her faith, Sheila navigates past death on at least three occasions, and valiantly blows past unrelenting pain and blatant blunders in the medical system. Be prepared to brace yourself when it gets intensely emotional.

I also advise you to hang on as she experiences: an unceremonious year as a California beauty queen; being slighted by the love of her life days after losing their unborn child; a heartless doctor who rather remove her reproduction organs than address her ruptured appendix, and driving alone across the San Francisco-Oakland Bay Bridge without being able to use the gas, or brake pedals in her car.

How she overcame these events—and others—will echo down through the ages.

But there's more than that to the story. You'll enjoy nostalgic glimpses of USC championship football; Hank Renner and Big

Time Wrestling, and summers in the south during the sixties.

You're going to love her memoir. It's not only going to make quite an impact on you, it offers arrestingly vivid memories and life-altering, lessons to enjoy and learn from.

I often think about the enormity of the amount of courage and strength her memoir is going to bring out of people. And that is why I wholeheartedly recommend this book.

This awe-inspiring narrative will leave you with an unexpected appreciation for everything that has ever come against you, and everything that ever will.

You'll see that through Sheila's high points and low points, at no point was God not there.

In writing the book, the author metaphorically prepares a path using "keep going" stepping stones. The purpose is to inspire all who come behind her.

Her life is the epitome of "just won't quit." Hopefully, it will always be that way.

Sheila Anthony-Shaw is an energetic, sixty-year-old who still has the same spark, infectious smile, and wisdom which were responsible for her being crowned Miss Fresno County forty years ago.

This is her story.

Fran Briggs
Community Relations Director &
Publicist to Sheila Anthony-Shaw

Introduction

"Wait. Wait. What's the rest of the story?"
I am awed by the number of times that question arises. It's always followed by my 60-second, elevator speech which explains why I walk with a cane. Quite frankly, it's a bizarre story.

Fifteen years ago, after being bitten by a soft-shell tick, I contracted a tick-borne disease (Tick-borne Relapsing Fever). It's an infection that compromises the body's blood, joints, and ligaments.

Initially, I wasn't prescribed the proper treatment. That caused the disease to spread and cause unrelenting, systemic pain throughout my whole body.

Today, I am still managing pain and am subject to losing my balance without warning.

After I present my speech it's apparent that although people are intrigued by my response, they still want to hear more.

They want to know why what's generally perceived as potentially bleak has neither halted my joy nor stopped my steps.

People listen to the energy that is attached to my words. It resonates with their spirit.

It seems so strange to most. They expect an absence of vitality.

The truth is it's never been my style to speak without passion. I know that each opportunity can be a gift to all who hear. What better way to honor God than with charismatic words and actions that mobilize people?

I was stricken by a debilitating disease that caused two types of infections which would linger on for thirteen years. But long before that, I knew God was preparing me to go through something, I just didn't know what.

The road to recovery was a journey that I absolutely could not have imagined.

What I do know is, just like you—God made me for a divine purpose. Therefore, whatever happens to me is aligned with that purpose.

Despite not being able to move as swiftly as I did fifteen years ago, I still maintain a natural, high-energy disposition. I am told by strangers and close friends alike that very few have the zest and zeal that I do.

I'm not only an enthusiastic optimist; I am a devout believer of Jesus Christ. However, you will more than likely find this book enjoyable no matter what your creed is.

This memoir was written with candor and charisma. It is both my history and my present. It's particularly interesting to people who enjoy being inspired, as well as learning from the lessons of others. My hope is that after reading this, you will have that same experience, too.

It illustrates how I sustained my positive outlook despite what I was up against. If you're struggling, I give you the fuel needed to get your life off the ground. In every case, I believe you'll be greatly moved by the way the story evolves.

You'll enthusiastically discover (or be reminded of) reasons to be liberated from your own fears and inhibitions. You'll be reminded that commitment and charisma can conquer even the most challenging circumstances.

Why am I sharing my story?
I share to honor and give glory to God. I share so that others may be healed and inspired to never concede. I share to celebrate, laugh and release my tears.

Finally, know that positive expectation and a healthy perspective plays a huge role and makes an incredible impact on how you live your life. These two factors will keep you grounded and elevated.

May my continuing journey inspire those who may have given up long ago; and those who seek additional inspiration.

God stilled the waters in my life. He can do the same for you.

Warmly,

Sheila Anthony-Shaw

*This book is dedicated to
my loving husband, Bryan
who has supported me through sickness and in
health.*

Mom and the Other Woman of Influence

T here are two women who have made the deepest impact in my life: my mother, Eula Mae Anthony; and my second-grade teacher, Ms. Johnson.

Both of these ladies were the epitome of sensibility; but more importantly, they left an impression that inspired me beyond measure.

Eula Mae was mom, to me. Before that, she was daughter to John Hampton Powell, and Elizabeth County-Powell. Mom was one of their twelve children who were born in the small community known as St. Maurice, Louisiana.

On June 21, 1925, Eula Mae was born in New Morning Baptist Church in St. Maurice. In the late 1930s, her family migrated to Conroe, Texas. After graduating from eighth grade the family moved to Houston, Texas.

In 1946, Eula Mae met, courted, and married Robert Lee Anthony. Through this union, the couple had five children. I am the third daughter, and fifth child. We were all born in Houston, Texas.

After Robert Lee Anthony's untimely death, my siblings and I were raised by our single mother. She did a wonderful job and had a huge influence in a family where the members truly loved each other.

One would think that raising five children on her own was a complex array of exhausting undertakings.

That was not the case for mom.

My siblings and I were well-disciplined. And, we were extremely close. Each of us supported the personal interests and activities of the others.

Mom was strong, kind, and dignified in all things. She was spectacular in the eyes of her children and others. She was my heroine.

Growing up in her household meant that God was first, and ethics actually meant something.

Our house rang with children's voices and laughter most of the day, every day. We were Mom's entertainment.

However, when she told us to outside and play, we *knew* it was time to go outside and play. She was trying to get something completed and needed a quiet house.

My siblings and I would retreat to our rooms, put on our play clothes, and immediately go outside and play.

Our city's irrigation canal was adjacent to our home. That meant we entertained many mosquitoes during the warm weather. Tragically, a few boys lost their lives trying to swim in the canal.

Incredibly, my brother Charles taught himself how to swim in the canal without being swept away by the strong undercurrents and turbulence.

I suppose that feat speaks to the level of his confidence and athleticism; but even more about the grace of God.

As a family we didn't have a lot. Quite frankly, we were poor. At least according to America's standard in the 1950s and 1960s.

However, I know that was part of the grand scheme of things. It helped us to remember where we came from, to always honor God, and to believe Him for our increase.

When things weren't going so well for her children, Eula Mae used repetition as a tool. She knew that repeating a scripture, nuggets of wisdom, and inspirational quotes was how most people learned best.

When I speak to my siblings about it today, we realize how much she wanted us to receive the promises, healings, and long life God reserved for us.

Mom taught us that when we decided to handle challenges without God, we were making things harder than they had to be.

She was a genius in planting seeds in her children's hearts and minds. She'd say, "God has a plan. Stop trying to fix this yourself."

I saw a new woman emerge from Mom every time she prayed without ceasing. When she did finish, she'd remind us that we all had access to God. One of the scriptures she quoted most often is from the book of Jeremiah.

For I know the plans I have for you," declares the Lord, "plans to prosper you and not to harm you, plans to give you hope and a future.

(Jeremiah 29:11, New International Version)

She'd always reminded us that God was aware of what was happening in our lives. He knew things we didn't know, even though we thought we did.

We also came to the conclusion that there was a reason mom prayed out loud. She was teaching us how to relate to God. As our Creator, God was forming us, but He also wanted a personal and intimate relationship with us. We were *His* kids, too!

Eula Mae Anthony encouraged her children daily and taught them that there was no limit on what they could accomplish.

I loved that.

Mom was wondrously connected to her children. She was sensible, had exceptional character, and always spoke with a great deal of reason.

She was a beautiful lady without pretense. And, she was decisively, firm. Her terms were non-negotiable.

Eula Mae Anthony was also stern. We weren't allowed to say "stupid" or "shut-up." She had enormous self-control and wanted to impart that trait into each of her children.

I remember the time when my brother Charles missed his curfew for being home. Our curfew meant that we were expected to be inside the house before the streetlights came on.

I don't recall if it was Charles' first time, but I am almost certain it was the last time he missed his curfew.

It seemed far-fetched to me that he would take such a risk, but so did climbing the fence and plunging into the city's irrigation canal when he wanted to swim.

On that particular evening when he didn't make curfew, his two close friends, Joe and Butch, were with him. That meant even his guests were locked out of the house.

Charles knocked, and even banged on the door, but his pleas and antics went unanswered.

A cool night on the porch eventually turned into a cold morning on the porch. That was the consequence for being disobedient. In my mother's eyes—and heart, her son's actions represented the utmost disrespect.

My mother gave all three of the boys something to wear. She was not a heartless woman. She would never leave them without something to cut the chill in the air that night.

However, it wasn't enough. The temperature dropped to the point where the trio became shivering-cold. Since they were without shelter, they needed to act quickly.

Ingenious as he was, my brother got the idea to make a make-shift bed to keep them all warm. Using the season's fallen leaves, and my mother's clean quilt which was hanging on the clothesline, Charles did just that.

When my mother opened the door to let them in the next morning, her eyes immediately became fixed on her quilt. It was on the dirty ground covering the boys and a bed of leaves.

There were no giggles. Mom was *furious*. So furious, she said nothing. My brother was excessively apologetic.

"I'm sorry, mom. I'm sorry, mom."

He rapidly repeated that numerous times. Realizing he needed to present a solution, he told her he would wash the quilt again, himself.

That same morning before going to school, Charles carefully washed and gingerly hung the quilt on the clothesline. When he came home from school that afternoon, he folded it up, and presented it to her.

That was a tough-love, lesson learned. It served to encourage the right behavior as well as to remind by brother to respect the expectations of the lady of the house.

When I was fourteen, my mother had an appointment. She instructed me to stay in the house. I was left in the charge of my sister in law who was at least five years older than me.

Well, it had to be 110 degrees that day in Fresno. I decided that I could ride my 10-speed bike to the local 7-Eleven convenience store. I knew that a bag of Lay's Barbecue Flavored Potato Chips and a bottle of soda would ease my discomfort.

I rationalized that, even though I would be riding in sweltering heat, it shouldn't be a problem since the store was just two blocks away.

Entering the store was divine. The cold, stream of air coming from the air condition was the perfect retreat from the heat. I would have stayed much longer, but I did not want to take that risk.

After I made my purchase, the clerk put my soda and potato chips into a bag, and then I walked out of the store and onto my bike.

I wanted to be safe and keep both hands on the handlebars as I rode home. That meant I would hold the bag in my mouth.

However, after a few seconds of clenching my teeth, the tension from my jaw muscles was too much. I realized how painful and awkward the ride back home would be.

I got off my bike and removed the items from the brown bag before discarding it.

Then, I with the bottle of Coke in one hand; and my small bag of potato chips in the other, I mounted the bike and with one push of my pedal I began the ride back home.

Things were going rather smoothly. I was looking forward to relaxing on my bed, enjoying my snack and listening to the radio.

Just as I peddled into our garage, I lost my balance, over-corrected, and fell off of my bike landing on my left side.

Immediately, I could see that the dark, carbonated beverage was no longer encased in the bottle.

Then, I noticed the blood. It was oozing out of my left arm.

I walked into my home. After seeing my arm and hearing what happened, my sister-in-law and I both agreed that a trip to the hospital was more than a great idea.

Since my mom was at one of the two hospitals in Fresno visiting her sister, we went to the other hospital. It was closer.

Twenty-one stitches and two hours later, I was back at home in my bedroom. The shot of novocaine the doctor gave me was wearing off. I didn't notice the pain until then. It was incredibly intensive.

My mom still was not home so I had time to think about what my punishment would be. There was *always* a consequence when we chose not to obey.

When my mom arrived home a short time later, she had a brief conversation with my sister-in-law. After hearing about what happened, she entered my room.

I was lying on my bed and listening to the radio. A propped pillow supported my injured arm. She approached me then examined my bandaged arm. I had no idea what she would say.

Never one to beat around the bush, Mom told me

that the gash in my arm, twenty-one stitches, and the accompanying pain was punishment enough.

There were no consequences for me that day--at least not from her.

"You are suffering from the consequences," Mom said.

She was remarkably on point.

The pain began to throb and become more intense due to the stitches in my arm.

Then, there was the time when my mom emphatically instructed my siblings and me to stay in our yard while she went grocery shopping.

Shortly after she left, my siblings had a better idea.

They thought our time could best be spent playing for hours at the local playground. I, being the youngest, followed along.

As we returned to the house later that afternoon, we could see from the distance that mom had a small branch from our weeping willow tree in her hand. We—and many kids back then—knew it as 'a switch.'

It made my older siblings giggle with embarrassment; however, it was not a laughing matter for my mom.

She figured that if her directions weren't enough to make an impression on why it was not a good idea to undermine her authority as our parent, a switch would.

Although mom only had an eighth-grade education, she was very smart. She taught me many things that confirmed and accentuated my sense of worth.

I supposed that's why I was never troubled by a lack of self-esteem.

As a devoted member of a Christian family, I was taught how to value each hour of every day I was given. They were gifts. Mom told all of children, innumerable times: 'Tomorrow is not promised.'

As a family, we learned how to delight in the small pleasures that were part of each moment of every day.

We also learned how to take nothing for granted.

My siblings and I were taught to express gratitude and be thankful for what we had. These were called our "blessings."

Our blessings were what the majority of people enjoy every single day; but for others, not at all. Our blessings included running water, electricity, food on our table, and arms to hug each other.

Knowing that there was a God who saw fit that my

family had what we needed was one of the many turning points in my life. It was one of my earliest illustrations that God is faithful.

Mom was a Proverbs 31 woman. That means she created a rich environment filled with songs of gratitude. She loved God, deeply.

I don't believe that there was ever a morning in my lifetime that mom didn't begin it with concentrated prayer while on her knees.

She was encouraging her children to do the same.

Her patience, discipline, respect for God, and work ethic became qualities I would adopt and make my own.

Our days were often graced with her singing songs of worship and praise. That's how she gave thanks unto the LORD. It was one of many seeds planted which helped me become the woman I am today.

Seeing her worship and praise God told me I could do the same. And when I did, I could hear what He was saying, and see what he was doing. He was rearranging things so miracles could come forth.

Eula Mae was greatly revered and admired for making the best of any situation. She was a gift to anyone who was in her presence.

For years, mom reminded us again and again, to step outside of our comfort zones and dismiss the perceived limitations others may have for our lives.

She also taught us to always be kind, but wise.

Mom would say, "Be cordial and polite; but know that you don't necessarily have to be everybody's best friend."

She was training us to treasure every relationship, even if every relationship was not necessarily a friendship.

Mom also taught us about the importance of forgiving—no matter how much we may be offended or disrespected.

We also learned what the purpose of work *really* was, and how important it is to be on time.

"You will work in a man's environment; but your work is for God," she'd say.

Eula Mae wanted us to spread our joy. She wanted us to be the light in dark places.

What she didn't want was for her children to be followers of men. So, she went to work and nurtured the leader that was inside each of us.

Today, as I reflect upon the souls of each of my

siblings, I see she was successful in that endeavor.

Eula Mae Anthony was also one of the most generous individuals I've ever known. Her heart and mind were always tuned into the needs of others.

Few would argue that mom took it upon herself to build a strong, welcoming home, neighborhood, and community. In her heart, everyone was worthy of love.

When my older brother played on the Edison High School football team, many of the players spent time at our home and often talked with my Mom.

How she managed to feed so many hungry, young men on such meager resources still amazes me today.

I do know that for this to have happened, she had to collaborate with God. That's why I am not surprised that everything she shared was always replenished.

This is what I know for sure: Mom could not have achieved such accomplishments unless God had provided through many.

The team, coaches, and their wives would often come by the house and drop off food. That was a sweet gesture. They knew Mom fed the community, regularly.

It was important to my mother to be an encouraging

influence on my brother, his friends, and the adults in their lives'. She wanted to set an example for future generations.

Mom made sure all of her children were safe and had their needs met. From that point, she would check in on the neighbors. She would regularly send them plates of food when they needed them, and even when they didn't.

They weren't just any plates, either. They were homemade, hot meals made with the same love she used to serve her children.

Whether it was food, or her time, mom served everyone with love largely because of this scripture.

... In everything; do it not only when their eye is on you and to curry their favor, but with sincerity of heart and reverence for the Lord.

(1 Colossians 3:22, New International Version)

Whenever mom did something that was foundational to our spiritual and personal growth, she would explain to her children why. She knew the time would come when they would have the same opportunity. I'm really glad she did.

My mom was very strong, but not invincible.

When I was in first grade, she became very sick and had to be hospitalized for six months. She was challenged by a thyroid condition which made it difficult to swallow.

Her doctor advised surgery. She adamantly but respectfully said, "No."

That was my Mom's way.

She had an enlarged thyroid. It's also known as a thyroid goiter. Thank God the lump on her neck was benign. That in no way meant that my mother wasn't in pain. I am sure she was; she just never complained.

Since surgery wasn't an option for her, she received rounds of radioactive treatment. While she was in the hospital, my oldest sister moved back home to take care of her siblings.

When you're a little girl who adores your mother, a month without living without her can be devastating.

Six months was almost unbearable.

When my siblings visited her in the hospital, I was not allowed in her room. I was too young.

Mom knew how much I wanted to see her, and I knew she wanted to see me. She managed to muster more than enough strength to leave her room and visit me in the lobby.

I was happy to see her and enjoyed every minute of our time together.

Eventually, she regained her health, vitality, and energy. The day came soon enough when she was discharged from the hospital, and back to enjoying life in her own home. That's where she was most comfortable.

Everything Mom did provided a useful framework for thinking about how I would engage with others in the future. I decided I would be just as loving and just as engaging when it came to family and strangers, alike.

Eula Anthony knew that joy from the LORD would manifest every time she did the right thing. The 'right thing' was what God expected from her.

In my family home was where I first learned that both kindness and a generous spirit were equally as important.

Eula Mae's words and deeds still guide me when I write and speak, today. She made my life meaningful and complete. She was a foundational example of God's sufficient grace.

No one knows everything about God. My Mom was not an exception.

I learned how to resign my own lack of understanding in many things by praying and giving the matter to God. My Creator is the only one to hear both my first and final plea.

I've never been one to nurture anxiety. I was groomed to be genuinely happy and content no matter what situation I may be in. Mom always said that things somehow always have a way of working out; and they do.

As I touched upon earlier, over the stove and near the oven is where my four siblings learned to cook. Our mother knew that these were invaluable life skills whether her children would marry, or not.

As for me?

Ha!

Cooking was neither a passion nor mandate. I gave myself a general exempt from the task. As a child, I decided I was going to be rich and my maid would do all the cooking.

Before every breakfast we could hear the sounds and sense the smells of something hot and hearty. Anything that she prepared—in no short order—was always incredible. It was absolutely delicious.

We enjoyed tasty, scrambled eggs, crispy bacon, or sausage, and toast that was actually toasted in the oven. A toaster in those days was a luxury item that wouldn't come to our home until a few years, later.

For lunch, we enjoyed a variety of delectable sandwiches, soups, or whatever mom would make available for us.

Dinner was very important. It was family time. I recall many nights when my all-season, athlete brother was not there either because he had a late practice or was traveling to a game.

Nevertheless, there was always a flavorful plate waiting for him in the oven when he came home.

One of my favorite dinners prepared by my Mom was crispy, delicious, golden fried chicken. It was always seasoned perfectly. The sides included greens or green beans, rice, and corn bread. Everything was cooked from scratch. All of it was *excellent.*

For dessert we enjoyed the likes of homemade, German-chocolate, cake. I savored every bite of anything that mom cooked or prepared because it was good.

Mom was an amazing seamstress, too.

When I reflect back, it is with pride to know that Eula

Mae Anthony sewed a lot. She was always getting complements. Her work was simply magnificent.

Sewing was one of her many gifts. She had a disciplined, attention for detail, and each garment reflected that. The task was never laborious. It was more like a hobby and she truly enjoyed it.

One of my favorite memories as a child was her sewing clothes for my *Julia* Barbie doll.

Who does that?

No one I knew, back then. Mom was a creative, and an ingenious creative at that. She encouraged me most with this original, powerful quotation:

"Faith in God will cover and protect; it may not be easy, but it's worth it."

– Eula Mae Anthony

I didn't know it then, but I know now that my mother was teaching me to rest in the grace of God. I accomplished numerous other feats with those words in mind. They are the impetus behind me founding Hs Mercy Ministry in Northern California.

Eula Mae's counsel—and that quote in particular, sparked a will for a life of ambitions and achievements for me. Cherished are her words with an affectionate remembrance.

I attribute God and Mom's counsel for me being the recipient of awards and honors from the Assembly California Legislature and the Congress of the United States House of Representatives. The honor was for outstanding leadership.

Pixley, California was a small community. The closest church was about twenty miles away from where we lived. That made it difficult to attend without a car; so, mom would host bible meetings at our house with our family. Anyone who wanted to attend was welcome.

My mother moved us two times to experience a better quality of life.

In 1962, when I was three, Mom moved us from Houston, Texas to Pixley. Her sister was living in the California city at the time. Mom wanted to raise her children where they could thrive.

The move from Houston, Texas to central California was a bigger adjustment for my siblings than it was for me. My oldest brother was sixteen years old. All of my siblings had established friendships and relationships to process through before saying goodbye.

In Pixley, the school system was smaller and in a few ways stronger. Also, the wages for domestic work in California were a bit higher than they were in Texas.

Our new California home was a one-room, wooden shack. The living space was tight. I will go as far as to say, crammed.

We didn't complain, though. There was absolutely no reason to. We adapted and enjoyed the adventure.

The floors were wooden slats. We could see the earth that was under our home. We had roll-out beds.

A roll-out bed is also known as a rollaway bed. It is a sturdy, metal frame with a mattress that folds in half. The bed frame had wheels on the bottom so it could easily and conveniently move to create more room during the day. That is how the five of us slept.

The shack did not have a bathroom. We used an outhouse which was ten steps from the home.

Our outhouse was a small structure which housed our toilet. They were in used in less-developed cities and towns that had no indoor plumbing. Today, similar structures are still used in certain rural and remote areas.

Taking baths was also an experience that only a small segment of America's population can relate to. Each of us bathed in a large, gray, oval, tin container.

That was our bathtub.

Store-bought bars of soap were not in the budget. Mom taught us how to use lye as a base to make our own soap. We didn't have the luxury of a water heater, either. The stove was used to create the wonderful experience of a hot bath.

The tin container we used to take our baths was multi-purposed. Coupled with a scrub board, it was also our washing machine.

After washing our clothes we'd put each garment through the wringer to squeeze out as much water as we could. The more water extracted from a garment, the faster the drying time.

It was laborious in nature but extremely efficient. The wringer removed almost twice as much water as the spin cycle does on an electric or gas dryer.

As you might imagine, getting heavy jeans through the wringer was a piece of work.

All of our clothes were dried on the clothesline as long as the weather permitted. Interesting enough, the washboard was also an instrument. I know this because

I come from a family of Louisiana zydeco enthusiasts.

Zydeco is a music genre. It evolved in southwest Louisiana by French Creoles and Native people in Louisiana in the beginning of the twentieth century.

Zydeco music blends blues, rhythm and blues, as well as music indigenous to Louisiana. The washboard was used in zydeco bands then, and is still used by bands, today.

This was our life when we first touched down in Pixley, California.

What struck me most about Pixley were the roads. Specifically, they were comprised of a fine, brown, powdered dust that had a tendency to cling to tires and shoes. You couldn't drive a clean car or walk barefoot without impunity.

This wasn't something that would be tolerated in our home. Each of us was expected to thoroughly dust off our shoes before entering.

After a few months of living in Pixley we moved to Fresno. It was literally a matter of life and death.

My oldest brother was battling "valley fever." It's a potentially fatal disease. Mom wanted him near medical facilities that could best serve him. Fresno, California offered that. It was our second move.

I mentioned earlier that there were two women who I recognize as being the most inspiring and making the deepest impact in my life. The second is the late, Ms. Johnson.

She was my second-grade teacher at Franklin Elementary School in Fresno. Ms. Johnson entered my life a few years after our family moved to Fresno.

To me, Ms. Johnson was the 'black, June Cleaver.' That is to say, if there ever was a black, Theodore "Beaver" Cleaver, Ms. Johnson would certainly be his mother.

Ms. Johnson and my mother both had tiny waists. However, unlike Mrs. Cleaver, my mom never owned a strand of real pearls.

They both were beautiful. The two were lady-like, kind, and greatly admired for their well-kept, look. They were the impetus behind my values presenting themselves, early.

Ms. Johnson was the kindest teacher and was very approachable. She fostered caring relationships with students, staff, and parents.

Even as a child, I knew that she truly wanted her students to succeed. She was very encouraging and smiled often.

I can still see her in my mind today gracing the classroom in beautiful, eye-catching dresses and high heels. Her hair is perfectly set in a French roll with bangs.

Her attire was always fashionable. In my eyes, she was elegant; and I admired her slender figure. As such, she didn't to have to wear a girdle. I wanted to grow up and have that same luxury.

Evidently, she was doing a lot of things right. After teaching a few years, Ms. Johnson became a highly respected, principal. She left this earth when she ninety-five years old.

In retrospect, I find it rather interesting that my intense adulation for these two women inspired my own identity.

A Better Life

In Fresno, mom found a church that she could be a meaningful part of. She was completely and unselfishly devoted to God in and out of church. Although she was not a formal leader, she did excel in community outreach as it pertained to representing our church.

Eula Mae was a humble servant. She was never one who strived to be part of the "in-crowd" at church—or anywhere for that matter. Her service and life were solely devoted to God.

Although I am pretty sure I would have picked up on her loving ways on my own, I'm not so sure that the passion and pride to do so would have been so fervent.

Mom strived to bring the teachings and promises from the Holy Bible to life. Although she was a single mother going through tests and trials, she persevered with the help of God.

I am especially and eternally thankful for her. She championed and helped shaped my life—as well as the lives of my siblings. Her character and judgment were memorable and impressionable.

God showed her the possibilities in her children's lives and she shared them with us. We saw, what God saw.

Ultimately, she knew God gave us all free will so far be it from her *not* to let us live our own lives.

Nevertheless, she taught us that most choices did not come without consequences.

We had a small church and an even smaller congregation. Everybody pulled their weight in honor of the LORD.

On Sundays we were in service most of the day. Sunday school started at 9:30 a.m. That was followed by a short break, then regular service from 11:00 a.m. until 1:30 p.m.

We would eat a light lunch and then hang out at nearby park before returning for the 3:30 afternoon service.

Under these circumstances, members had multiple roles and responsibilities. One could be the usher and in the choir; another would facilitate Sunday school, and receive the collection.

A church member could attend a missionary board

meeting and have choir practice on the same evening.

Mom was extremely active in her roles. She did a lot of work in the organizing fundraisers, cooking meals, and even refurbishing the church.

In 1970, I recall mom overseeing the fish and chicken dinner fundraisers. I watched her and learned how she led.

Community members could either buy a fish or chicken dinner for six dollars. The meal included a generous portion of food and sides such as green beans, cornbread, and black eye peas.

I remember selling can sodas to go along with the meal for fifty cents each.

Mom was a devoted servant. Unfortunately, members were expected to rely on the pastors of the church, and not the LORD of their lives. We were not taught how to build a personal relationship with God.

The emphasis was put on learning God's word so members could pull it out when they needed it, as opposed to seeking the Creator who desires to speak and commune with all of His children.

All was not lost. Years later, mom would learn that a pastor's role was to help its congregation enhance their personal relationship with God.

I recall one particular Sunday morning when I was nine years old. My heart heard a sermon that touched me deep down in my soul. My pastor was teaching about the importance of being obedient to both God, and our parents.

As I listened, I knew this was something I wanted to honor with all of my heart. The pastor continued sharing how God wants us to behave, and if we chose to do so, long life as a child of God would be our "free gift."

Upon hearing those words, I enthusiastically ran to the altar. I wanted Jesus in my life. I wanted a *new* life. And I wanted the "free gift" known as salvation. God gave me just what I needed that morning.

I received a new life, hope, joy, and salvation. Today, I live completely with God's compassion. With a dose of realism mixed with imagination and humor, I know that with God, all things are possible.

I was baptized when I was twelve-years-old in that church. I attended faithfully for thirty-five years.

Through God's word I aim to share my faith with those who desire a closer relationship with Him. I dedicate and live my life so that the ministry that God gave me is sustained long after I leave this earth.

My desire is to fulfill God's will and purpose. I will

continue to enhance the lives of all who God puts in my path. I decided long ago to see every opposition as an opportunity.

Mom was never in the military, but she certainly had a military mindset when it came to responsibilities and discipline. She made the most out of all the opportunities to keep her children on their toes. This was part of our grooming.

What set Mom apart from most people from any other generation was that she 'walked her talk.' The two went hand-in-hand. There wasn't one thing that was even remotely hypocritical about her.

All who knew or met Eula Mae Anthony saw how disciplined she was. They witnessed her expressing the purpose of her life, and her utmost respect and love for God.

She was heaven-bound and invited countless people to join her along her journey.

As far as I can remember I was always engaged and involved with my mother. She lovingly, freely, and effortlessly gained my attention.

I spent a considerable amount of time with her. She invested a lot of time in me. Mom taught me how much Jesus loved me. And she taught me how to rest in Jesus.

Eula Mae Anthony was employed as a domestic. She made her living by cleaning and cooking for others. In or out of our home, she worked unto God tirelessly and with perfection.

She was gracious and compliant. Her employers respected her for being so.

During the evenings which she prepared more food than an employer's family would eat, she was allowed to bring what was not needed, home. The last of that delicious meal became dinner for her children.

My mother learned a lot about how well-to-do families lived and entertained. She taught her daughters all the things that are required to host a memorable dinner party.

I learned everything from how to position place settings and serve the food; to how to set the ambiance and plan a menu.

Although she was a domestic, Eula Mae was always stylish, neat, and clean. She was divinely-free from any tendency to be slothful.

Her skin was absolutely beautiful. It was smooth, flawless, and without wrinkle. These are just some of the thousands of defining elements that set prevailing tones and memories for me.

Mom was a lady. Growing up, I was groomed to be lady-like too; but without dismissing the Lion in me—spiritually-speaking, of course.

Today as I progress through life, I know that without a doubt, what happened in my past shaped me for my present and future.

For instance, as long as I can recall I've been compelled to look out for those who may need something. When I see these souls, I approach them and offer what I can.

Reaching out and offering a much-needed hand at just the right moment brings me sheer joy.

Do nothing out of selfish ambition or vain conceit. Rather, in humility value others above yourselves, not looking to your own interests but each of you to the interests of the others.

(Philippians 2: 3-4, **NIV**)

This next scripture speaks to my heart.

It was one of my mother's favorite scriptures that she modeled most of her life:

...Whenever you eat or drink ...do it all to the glory of God.

(1 Corinthians 10: 31, **NIV**)

The memory that leaves the most impact is how my mother promoted and prepared each of her children for self-reliance.

She was outstanding at it.

She cooked, cleaned, sewed, iron, and taught her children how to do the same—even the boys.

What an amazing woman she was. She made all of her clothes. Mom was an excellent cook who took pride in preparing delectable meals.

She also was an incredible food manager. She would purchase in bulk when she could, and that almost always made sense.

Eula Mae prepared meals in ways in which they would go the furthest. I suppose that made her an excellent food manager, too. We were never hungry.

There were many occasions in California when my mother and two of my aunts would jointly purchase an entire cow or pig. That was a common thing that families or friends did.

Then, they would cut and share the meat between the three, respective households. Not only was the meat prepared in more ways than one could imagine, it would last for months in our deep freezer.

School

I didn't go to preschool. My first formal year of education was as a kindergartener. At this level, there are almost no previously established, peer connections.

If you weren't affiliated with a church or neighborhood, or if you didn't recognize any familiar faces, you made friends from scratch.

On the playground from a short distance, I saw a few girls laughing as they were playing on a slide. One of the girls made eye contact with me and smiled. Then without hesitation, she skipped towards where I was standing.

"Hi, do you want to play with me?"

That made me smile a little bigger.

I am not sure if I even got the opportunity to say, "Yes." The girl just grabbed my hand and led me to her friends where we all began to play together. Joy was my very first friend from school.

Even though Joy and I went on to attend different middle and high schools, we continued to stay in touch and remain friends. She's very dear to me. Her heart is so big.

We have never once talked negatively about others. We enjoyed fun, girlfriend sessions that were designed to support each other in whatever we were going through at the time.

Amazingly, fifty-five years later, a lady walked past me in church. I was living in Northern California at the time. She looked so much like my friend, Joy. The resemblance was incredible.

At some point from a short distance, we eventually made direct eye contact. It was my friend Joy!

We exchanged smiles. I was beyond thrilled. She was, too. We both were there to enroll in a bible study class that same day.

Growing up, I loved school. Largely because I love people and enjoy learning. Unfortunately, lying below the surface of the charm of school was an issue that runs ramped around the world today—bullying.

My fourth grade year was the beginning of my 'stand up for those who are bullied campaign.'

It didn't matter that I was the one being bullied at the

time.

I was thinner than most other fourth graders. I was picked on by my peers most of the year—but not because of my size. I was targeted because of my features.

I had big eyes. They were much larger than my classmates. And, my skin was darker than any of the other students.

I had never been the subject of torment of this nature before. This was all new to me, but I knew exactly why it was happening.

It was the first time that I attended a school that had very few people whose skin looked like my own.

As a matter of fact, there were only six African Americans in the entire school. I went from a predominantly black school, to a predominantly white school.

Did I mention it was in the 1960s?

That was a social experiment in itself.

During our lunch period, I was a loner who made a point to stay away from kids who would readily call me names and tease me.

It was a confusing era in my life. I was told that I was

very pretty and had beautiful eyes as much as I was told I was too dark and had bug eyes.

This was also the first time I recall being called, "Oreo."

When I asked why, I was informed because I was black on the outside but talked, "white."

That hurt me, but it didn't devastate me. I was friendly and made friends easily. It is in my spirit to be forgiving and treat others the way I would prefer to be treated.

Many have said that I have a gift to draw the best out of men, women, and children. I know within everyone there is brilliance and gifts which can be used to better our world.

Besides, there were more than a handful of students and teachers who genuinely saw me as a person—and not a color.

By the time I entered junior high school, I was able to immediately resonate with kids who were loners. Partly because it took me back to my fourth grade year as a loner, and partly because I remember how good it felt when Joy came across the yard that morning and invited me to play when in kindergarten.

When I saw a kid eating alone at lunch, I would

immediately approach them. I had an idea of what they might be feeling. It didn't matter that their skin was not black.

One day I noticed a boy across the yard. The playground ranged with children's laughter. It appeared that the boy distanced himself several yards from the voices of the other students. If that's what he preferred, he did a terrific job of not showing it.

I wasn't sure if he was craving to belong but was afraid to do so; or if he feared being bullied, teased, or rejected.

What I did know was that he represented millions of children and adults who were worthy of company, love, and acceptance.

I walked across the playground and approached him.

"Hey. You're with us; come on over."

That is how I would invite students who were by themselves to eat lunch with me and my friends.

Although some people prefer eating by themselves, I thought classmates should never eat alone. After all, we're all connected.

Sometimes, the response would be, "No, I'm okay; I'll just eat my lunch over here."

To that I would respond, "Okay."

However, the next day I would approach them again. This time I would ask, "Do you mind if I sit next to you and have lunch?"

They would usually respond, "No, not at all."

So, I sat and we would talk about classes, what elementary schools we came from, and what we liked to do for fun. If there was a point during our engagement that the kid would stop speaking, I would stop speaking, too. I wanted them to be at ease.

I've never been shy. Nor have I ever been intimidated to the point where I did not express my feelings using words. However, I do respect those who are not as adept in verbal communication.

I also recognize boundaries and will not knowingly cross them without permission. That's why I asked 'light and airy' questions such as, "What are you going to do this weekend?" I wouldn't push them to respond, but I would let them know that they were 'one of us.'

These were some of my ways to let someone know that we *all* are on the same team. I didn't know it then, but that was the genesis of my 'protect the underdog' campaign.' It would continue into high school, and beyond.

Summers in Houston

Mom knew it was not only important for her children to remember where they came from, but to know the family who still lived there.

At least three times, she escorted my sister Anne and me to Houston. There we would enjoy a month of summer with our Texas family.

My first trip to Houston was in 1968. It was made possible by a Greyhound bus ride. Riding the Greyhound bus was far less expensive than flying.

Mom packed enough food for the three of us. She was quite strategic and brought along food that people didn't mind eating cold. We didn't have the convenience of a microwave when we took breaks.

My Mom's cold, fried chicken was actually very good. The three of us also enjoyed hot dogs, homemade ginger cookies made with molasses, cornbread, and a thermos full of water. Each item was carefully wrapped and preserved in aluminum foil.

We also packed products designed to repel mosquitoes in the hot and humid region. Mosquitoes were notorious that time of year.

I suppose I will always remember these summer Greyhound bus trips. Mostly because the three-day, each-way trips were incredibly hot.

Actually, they were *tortuous.*

The closer we got to Houston, the more humid it became. I realize that after returning to the bus during a break in driving, I was never cooled to the point where I felt comfortable.

Many people might have been as uncomfortable as I was riding a bus with inadequate, air condition system. But there is value in the experience. It fostered appreciation for adequate, air condition environments.

The temperature stayed between 107 and 111 degrees.

At least that's what it felt like.

The bus made several stops during our trip. Passengers could leisurely get off the bus for breaks, while the bus driver loaded new passengers and luggage, and assisted those who reached their destination.

It was very exciting seeing the different landscapes and states that led to Houston. Arizona was scenic. I was captivated by the cactus and majestic mountains.

We drove through small towns along the way—much smaller and incredibly more rural than Fresno. We also traveled through Las Cruces, New Mexico, Texarkana, Dallas, before reaching Houston.

It was a *very* long trip.

When our bus arrived at the Houston bus station, we all were exhausted, but excited. One of my uncles was there to greet us and bring us to my grandmother's home. I could tell by the conversation he had with Mom that we were going to have fun.

I was so excited to see my grandmother. Just getting to know her was a treat. I could see my Mother in her so much.

I had uncles, aunts, and cousins to look forward to spending time with as well. But I was most thrilled about seeing and spending time with my mother's mother.

Upon entering the house, my sister and mom exchange big hugs. Everybody was happy to see everybody.

I am sure I saw them before we left Houston to move

to California; however, I was only three at the time. That was too young for me remember them.

And it really didn't matter. They were my family and now that I was old enough, I would simply make new and vivid memories.

My Aunt Mary lived directly next door to my grandmother. Behind my grandmother were two houses. One of my uncles and aunt lived in each of them. We spent the majority of the time in my grandmother's home.

It was so much fun meeting and getting acclimated with my cousins. We talked, giggled, and played like most cousins who enjoy each other do.

Occasionally, my grandmother would give each of the cousins a quarter. That brought a smile to our faces. I was not alone in my affection for sweets.

We would use that quarter to go to the store to buy penny-candy or whatever else that fixed our fancy and budget.

On our way to the store, I realized that the Houston heat was decisively humid.

No, *horribly* humid.

It was nothing like the dry heat we had in Fresno.

The worst part was that the sun seemed to grow hotter with each step. After a few seconds in the humid heat we began perspiring.

My cousins seemed to be acclimated with the humidity. It didn't seem to bother them as much.

As we walked, we chose to venture through a cemetery. We didn't have to; but it was a shortcut—and a dramatic one at that.

One of my cousins led us all to the side of the curb which led to a pathway that would take us through the cemetery. A mix of fright and giggles had our hearts racing.

She explained that after she said, 'Ready, set, go,' we would all take off together and run as fast as we could until we ran through the cemetery.

I would liken the experience to being similar to the scariest ride at an amusement park.

When the time came to announce, 'Ready, set, go,' we ran like mad until we got to the other side. As we did, we hoped that we would not be so loud as to disturb the residents.

We huffed and puffed as we walked a few yards more. I could see the store in the distance. I followed my cousins inside. It was a beautiful sight to behold.

There was an assortment of penny-candy.

Among our choices were: Taffy, Bit-O-Honey, Jolly Ranchers, SweeTarts and many more options to choose from.

On top of the counter in a tall, glass jar was the popular, giant pickles.

Delicious.

It was a favorite for children and adults when I was growing up.   It was the perfect snack.

Eating it was fun because every bite came with a good crunch which was immediately followed by vinegar brine. I believe it was sold for .35 cents during that time.

There's nothing more special than the chance to play with cousins you only see once a year. The time spent in Houston provided plenty of opportunities.

Some of my favorite childhood memories involve my family's annual trips to visit my extended family. The little pleasures I experienced still mean so much, today. My visits were almost everything I could have hoped for.

Almost.

The cool air never did make it during our stay.

My Bond with Mom

At home with Mom, I was particularly focused and enjoyed learning about God and the stories in the bible. I also enjoyed creating.

When my siblings left for school, were away with their friends, or simply aged out of the house, Mom and I would create together.

It mattered not if she was scrubbing floor, preparing a table, or organizing a function, she always performed any task with a tremendous amount of detail.

My one-on-one times with her were very special. She was very attentive when I spoke with her. In many ways, it was as if I was her only child. I knew I was every bit as special as I felt.

There were countless Saturday mornings when we would get up and enjoy breakfast and great conversation together. After that, both of us would clean the house.

It wasn't laborious at all for me; although I must

admit, Mom did most of the work.

When we were finished, we'd talked about many subjects. My absolute favorite thing to do on Saturday mornings was to lie across my bed and listen to the radio with my Mom as we chatted.

Mom also liked to relax by watching television.

Big Time Wrestling was her go-to program on Saturday afternoons. I didn't care too much for it, but I would join her.

The likeable and funny, Hank Renner was the move-to-move, announcer. It was a time when television wrestling was less flamboyant.

There was still the fan-favorite vs. the villain, but the glitter and other hoopla was absent.

Pepper Gomez was her favorite wrestler. She'd root for him every time he had a match. He was very handsome and had amazing muscles—especially his abdominal set. Pepper was known on the program as "The Man with the Cast Iron Stomach."

I loved the bond with mom. I wanted to always feel close to her. We genuinely had fun together. My memories of her will never fade.

When Mom counseled me, it was always bible-based. That was our compass. Clearly, she was preparing me for hurt, disappointments, and rejection. Not in a warning sense; but rather, in a blessed assurance sense.

"When you have a problem, give it to Jesus," advised Mom. "No matter what it looks like, He knows exactly what to do. Jesus can take something horrible and make it beautiful."

She'd often tell me, "God is going to use you for something mighty."

When I would see her friends, they would make the same statement to me. I was amazed by that and always accepted it to be the absolute truth. More importantly, there was plenty of evidence to that effect.

When money was short, Mom would never ask or borrow money from anyone.

Never.

Instead, my mother would make her mouth-watering cakes, pies, and other desserts and my aunt and uncle helped her sell them.

Things always worked out. She knew God would provide. I could see that God was a provider of great ideas, too.

Eula Anthony was an "envelope mom." That was the name mothers used for keeping their allowance money for bills, food, and other provisions organized by using a standard envelope.

When an envelope went dry, that meant there was no more immediate monetary provision for that specific purpose. It helped keep her on track and prevented overspending.

My Mom wasn't a very good dancer. The rhythm bone wasn't part of her skeleton. Nevertheless, we felt the passion and excitement of the music and her relationship with it. This was a meaningful part of the relationship we shared.

The relationship was closely woven and intricate. Our shared interests naturally ignited passionate conversation. I began to feel more anchored with her as I discovered who I was becoming, and our relationship grew in meaning, daily.

"Sometimes you're not going to understand why people behave or say what they do," she explained. "Just remember that we serve a God who is taking care of things. His grace is sufficient."

Pearls of wisdom like that have stayed with me. They guide and comfort me to this day.

Mom and I would discuss my future. I reminded her

that I wanted to become a lawyer. I wanted to focus on that. I was not going to cook and would pay someone to do so for me.

She admired my ambition but knew skills were important. Knowing how to take care of myself was just as important.

Knowing that I had a mother that loved God, and knowing God loved me meant my footing in the world would never be uncertain. Even if I did slip, I knew I would have a soft place to land.

High School

I loved high school. I was pleased with my academic and social experiences.

In our home, speaking slang and cussing were not allowed. My mom didn't use bad language and she expected her children not to use it either. Mom had zero tolerance for derogatory speech.

My brother Jessie could cuss like a sailor—but he never did it in front of my mom. I always wondered how he could control it.

I struggled socializing with other African American girls. Mostly because I adopted my own belief: speaking slang will never get anyone a job. It's best to get ready for your future and speak like a professional, now.

My peers told me I spoke "too white."

I responded, "What does that mean? Are you saying because I don't cuss or use slang means I speak too white?"

When I went home that day, I talked to my Mom about it.

"Don't listen to them; I didn't send you to school to use slang or cuss words."

And that was that.

My brother Charles is six years older than me. I was in junior high school when he attended college at the University of Southern California (USC).

One of my fondest memories of seeing him play was when I went with one of my girlfriends to the Rose Bowl. USC played Ohio State, and USC won. We had so much fun that day.

Even if you lived in Fresno, the Rose Bowl Game in Los Angeles (Pasadena, California) was one of the hottest tickets in town. The football game is typically played on New Year's Day at the Rose Bowl stadium.

Since 1945, it has been the highest attended college football bowl game. Most famously, it's a part of the Pasadena Rose Parade.

I was so excited during Charles' entire football career. He gave our family something else to be proud about. What I admired more than his talent was his humbleness.

This was an exciting time in our lives. As the younger sister of a professional football player, I effortlessly met and got to know a lot of the boys at my school who had a passion for professional football.

The boys at my high school knew Charles was my brother and most of them loved football. That made it relatively easy to engage in conversation.

They'd go out of their way to find me and discuss the game on Sunday; and Monday Night Football that following Tuesday.

Although I had no interest in being the popular girl, it was really fun to be well-known. I enjoyed football, but really wanted to be a cheerleader.

Unfortunately, I never made the squad during the three years that I tried out.

It was a strange sequence of trials. I was told and believed I had the talent and attributes to be a cheerleader. My peers were more shocked than I was when I didn't make the squad. More than one mouth was agape as each one approached me in disbelief. They thought for sure that I would be chosen.

I was cordial and had charisma as well as spark. I just couldn't connect with the cheerleader coordinator. The sad thing is that to this day, I have no idea why. I never took it personally, and it didn't steal my joy.

In high school, I was becoming a young lady. My Mother was especially strict during my high school years, but I didn't mind. I loved the structure and safety she provided.

Unlike my peers, if I had a midnight curfew, I was okay with leaving a party or an event by eleven. My girlfriends didn't understand that frame of thought at all. For them, leaving at eleven was leaving before the *real* fun started.

I loved having fun; but I loved structure, too. My mother was protective, but she wasn't over-protective. She didn't have to threaten me to be home on time. That wasn't her nature. If I was not home on time, there would be a consequence.

I also knew that my Mom would not sleep soundly until I was home and safe. Most teenagers don't consider this, or they are totally oblivious to it.

Socially, I have always been very secure. Even though I was a "social butterfly," I've never been one to cave into peer pressure.

Not having a boyfriend was perfectly okay with me, too. Although boys were cute, I wasn't into the things that many high school boys do.

I had so much freedom living at home without sharing it with children of my own, or a boyfriend. I enjoyed each moment of it.

I wasn't into drinking, either. As a matter of fact, I
didn't care for drugs at all. And, I didn't like seeing girls
who did. I wanted them to have a little more respect
for their bodies.

My Sensational Siblings

As the youngest of the family, I was the recipient of most of the perks that typically come with that status. Thirteen years separate me from my oldest brother. At the time of this writing, I am sixty, and my oldest brother is seventy-three.

Growing up, there was never a dull moment for the Anthony children. We took pleasure in what we needed most—each other.

Those who know us would describe us as outgoing, enthusiastic, and charismatic achievers who did different things but blended well with each other.

We didn't argue as most siblings do. It wasn't part of our spirit. Besides, Mom wouldn't tolerate it.

And, we never passed anyone who was going in our same direction. We made a point to speak to and greet all along our path.

We are loving and compassionate social-lights—courtesy of Eula Mae Anthony.

All of my siblings loved the LORD. We were a tightly-knit group that brought unique experiences to our household.

But we could also finish each other's sentences.

I have two brothers. Each time I got married one of them walked me down the aisle. That was pretty special.

Jesse Anthony

Jesse Anthony is the oldest. He is a retired auto mechanic and truck driver who lives in Houston, Texas. He's also a talented race car driver who has raced for more than five decades.

Cars have always been his passion. God continues to give him ideas to add to his amazing and creative mind. If Jesse can see it in his mind, he can do it.

Jesse developed a creative approach to prosper: do what you love.

So, he built a Corvette and drag racing car from the ground up. It was quite interesting how he did it; but not at all surprising that he did it.

He searched for and removed parts from old cars. Then, he pieced them together. It didn't matter if each car was a different model, make, or year.

From this point, he welded the parts together to create the most amazing vehicle that I have ever seen anyone drive.

It seems that he has always been ambitious, entrepreneurial, and willing to help others. He still works on cars today.

When he lived in California, Jesse loved competing at Fresno's Madera Speedway and raced innumerable times. Madera Speedway was small town, NASCAR racing. The Speed Way was where everybody hung out on Friday nights.

Jesse was very active at the speedway. He helped build a car and work with a friend who raced the vehicle there. His team broke the qualifying record, twice while competing. Each qualifying achievement determines your car's position in the race. It's very similar to the positioning of a relay race.

My brother is formally and self-taught. He can pretty-much solve any technical problem relative to any vehicle. I've never bought a car without consulting him, first.

God gave him knowledge, aptitude, and vision which you can't get from a book. He has a gift—an ability to go deep inside and orchestrates his brain to teach him how to problem-solve and trouble shoot.

I've always been a big fan of my brother because I think there's nothing he can't fix. He amazed mechanics and everyone in the auto racing world with his vision and skills.

Jesse is still an active operator of his own repair shop. His favorite hobby is still Friday night drag racing and hanging out with the guys in the pit.

He loves helping others, building cars, speed and racing. When I asked him how fast he has ever raced, he smiled and said, "Oh, maybe One-hundred-and-thirty miles per hour, or even a little faster. I'm not sure."

When he was about thirteen, my family lived in Pixley, California my siblings attended school in Delano California. It was about forty to fifty-mile school bus ride from our home.

There, Jesse attended classes for agriculture and amazed the teacher by drawing, building, and welding his very first vehicle. It was a utility trailer.

His teacher was just astounded by the 15-year-old who had an ingenious mind and ability to build a piece of farm equipment.

Jesse was offered grants to work on projects at school and given books to read to enhance education. Every teacher my brother met was always amazed by his ability to see and do things.

Some teachers admitted that they did not know how to do what Jesse, did.

When our family moved to Fresno, California, Jesse attended Edison high school along with my other siblings. He was immediately drawn to the auto mechanics classes that were offered.

One day, Jesse contracted Valley fever and became quite ill. He was hospitalized long enough that he was assigned a tutor in the hospital. Jesse described him as a very caring, teacher.

The tutoring was timely. It helped Jesse complete the requirements for his high school diploma so that he could graduate with his class. Miraculously, Jesse was healed from Valley Fever.

Although this incident happened to him and it seemed to cut things short, God's plan was much bigger than he could have ever imagined.

God saw fit to see Jesse live a life of helping and supporting and sharing his talents with others.

I've always been very proud of him. Today, Jesse lives a healthy life in Texas.

Jean Coward

My sister, Jean is the older of my two sisters. She is what I describe as super-smart and processes things, very quickly. She is a homemaker, bible study teacher, and retired librarian for the school district.

Jean was like a mom to me--especially during the difficult time in our lives when our mother was very ill. Jean was there for every single football game I've ever cheered at. She was also near me during every beauty pageant I've ever entered.

She has never missed any of my birthdays. I really appreciate my sister for being the woman that she was all while raising her five children, working, and attending school. She was and still is what I call, *my phenomenal woman.*

After returning to school, Jean earned her A.A. degree at the City College of Fresno, California. She did this as a librarian for Fresno Unified School District. She was always on the Dean's List.

In 1992, she attended Cal State University, Fresno. She received her degree in liberal studies, with an emphasis on education. Jean's passion for life mirrors her stamina. She worked for the Fresno Unified School District for approximately forty-four years.

She is an incredibly smart woman. I've always felt like she could read and comprehend anything, and then effortlessly apply what she read.

Jean is also a loyal friend and generously gives to others. We always had family dinners together and Jean would cook. She's excellent at this craft.

Jean loves books, lunch, and children. Those who know you will tell you that she's quite the perfectionist. Whatever she does, she does with class and style. There's elegance in the task and it's never half done.

She's artistic and has impeccable style. We all agree that she is very much like our mother. There's no doubt that mom made quite an impression. Jean performs innumerable tasks exactly the way Mom did.

Oh, and she won't run *anywhere.*

I guess I get those qualities from both her and my mom. I have learned about life and etiquette from both of them.

My sister is also an avid sports enthusiast. She has all the sports channels on her television so that she can watch everything at once. She is fascinated with the split screens, option and utilizes it often.

She never misses the tennis match. The William sisters—Venus and Serena—are her absolute, favorites. Jean loves most sports. I have had the pleasure of attending several professional basketball games with her.

My sister, Jean is the only woman I know who can read a book on tennis, and then coach a first-year team to the championship.

Interesting enough, while working for the school district as a librarian for many years, she was informed of a head coaching position for a girls', after-school, tennis team.

It was a new program. Apparently, nobody wanted to take on the responsibility of the practices, training, and working with the tennis team

Immediately, she set her mind and heart on becoming the new coach. She read several books from the library, and combined what she already knew about the sport, then took the position of head coach. Lo and behold, her team started winning their tournaments.

Everybody was flabbergasted. Here was a woman who never picked up a tennis racket, let alone play tennis. Yet, she was able to work with a group of young and talented children and bring out their strengths. I would have to say that this is her 'claim to fame.'

She inspires children, raises their positive self-esteem, and helps them to become the very best that they can be at something that nobody else thought they could do. For forty-four years, I've had the pleasure to watch her pour into the lives of others.

These are all illustrations that our talents are not our own. They are gifts given to us, from God. His intention is that we share our gifts with one another.

Today, she lives in the same town as her former students. Occasionally, both of my sisters run into children they used to teach who are in company of their own children. The parents honor my sisters each meeting and convey the love and support they received from their former teachers.

Anne Anthony

My sister, Anne is the third of four of my siblings. She is a wonderful mother of two daughters, and five grandchildren.

Growing up together, she and I stayed home longer than any of our other siblings. I supposed that's why we are the closest.

Anne was especially loving and cared for me when I was little. She walked me to and picked me up from school every day. She'd even walk me home for lunch, and then she would walk me back to school.

Anne was kind, protective, fun, and had the most infectious laugh. She has always showed love and graciousness towards me. Today, we're still very close and talk all the time.

Just as we did as children, we laugh at all sorts of things. We're so much alike.

For example, we'll buy the exact clothes, snapshot pictures of the items, and then and exchange pictures with each other. This tickles us so much. We realize our taste is keenly similar.

Anne didn't graduate from the Fresno high school she started at because we moved. She adapts well and made new friends. She's an extremely loving, kind, and supportive person.

She worked for her local school district for more than forty years. Although she is retired, she occasionally works as a substitute for the district. She enjoys spending time with the students, seeing them grow up, and move forward in life.

Anne is especially unique because she has a gift of making the most delicious desserts anyone could ever enjoy. Ironically, she doesn't care for sweets at all. I find that fascinating.

Our family's favorite desserts include her Snicker doodle cookies, and chocolate chip brownies with ice cream.

To avoid squabbles over her tasty desserts, Anne

divides and then places the cookies into decorated lunch bags which have our names on them.

Anne is very crafty; when I say this she bakes, decorates, designs, cooks, and sews. She takes old things and thinks up ideas of how to make something new out of it. For example, she'll take bathroom shower tiles and make decorative coasters.

She covers them with the stickers by using a paste. Then she uses a brush to shellac it.

Ta-da!

The final product is a set of attractive, shiny, personal coasters.

Among the most amazing things she has made are sweater pillows. She takes an old t-shirt and sews it up into a square. She leaves an opening to put a pillow inside. Finally, she sews the opening and ties the arms of the pillow.

I know for sure that my sister loves the Lord with all her heart. She dedicates her time to others and shares her gifts with many. She serves on committees, supported all my endeavors. She makes friends everywhere she goes and she's always fun.

I know most people don't have a family like mine, and this is why I deem it important to share my amazing gift with everyone. We serve a God who uniquely designed a specific purpose for all of us.

In (Psalm 139:14) I praise you because I am fearfully and wonderfully made; your works are wonderful. I know that full well.

That when He made my family, He gave each of us that unique design and gift that was made just for us individually, that no one else has or can use the way we do. I love that my family utilizes their talents to support and create.

Charles Anthony

My brother, Charles loves sports. As a child, he was on the field or track every day except Saturdays. That was the day when he was mowing, doing laundry, or sewing on buttons.

In addition to football, he also played baseball and ran track.

He was the athlete of the family. If he had it his way, he would have played all three major sports offered in high school.

However, my mom suggested that he choose two sports to participate in, and school came first.

Charles is a very talented individual. In high school

he excelled in football, baseball, and one year of freshman basketball.

Throughout the city and county, he was known for his unbelievable speed for his size for a middle linebacker. He played junior varsity football for a short period of time before being promoted to varsity.

Charles was always a leader and very-much respected by his teammates. He was chosen to be captain of his high school football team. This leadership role came with much responsibility. It meant that he was required to do things correctly and respectfully.

In 1969, he led Edison High School to the North Yosemite League Championship.

This caused a lot of frenzy in our household. That's because Charles didn't consider going to college as a life option. Suddenly, he was part of a bustling, recruiting process.

The high school coaches came to our home spoke with my mother and explained the pros and cons of the opportunities that were being presented to my brother.

His grades were exemplary, so that qualified him for a full scholarship to almost any top school in the country.

The coaches' role was to help Charles obtain a full

scholarship to the college of his choice. The whole process was amazing. Our household was bombarded with coaches from across the country.

Each coach took my brother and my mom to dinner in an effort to convince them that their college and academic program was the best avenue for his future.

Of course, today there are scholastic rules that restrict such courting. When I think of the process now, it reminds me of the movie Blindside (2008) which portrayed the life of NFL star, Michael Oher.

God blessed my brother with amazing ability, grit, and gifts. Eventually, he chose and was signed by the University of Southern California (USC Trojans).

Impressively he was in the starting lineup as a first-year, freshman. This was almost unheard of back then.

His 6'1", 230-pound frame, massive strength, and incredible speed impressed the USC coaches. Especially during a play when Charles knocked a player's helmet sideways while tackling him.

Charles says that God gave him his talents and designed him to be a unique person who stands out in any crowd.

While attending USC, he played in, and won two Rose Bowls. He acquired two rings for his accomplishments.

Later, Charles was drafted by the NFL and played professional football for the San Diego Chargers. He also played in the Canadian Football League for the BC Lions.

Today (2019), the retired, NFL linebacker, and former Heisman trophy candidate is the vice president of the NFLPA.

At the time of this publication, my siblings and I are all still very close and make time to speak to speak with one another at least once a week.

Francis John Coward

Francis is not one of my biological brothers, but he has been a big brother to me since I was seven-years-old.

At the time, our families were very close and he and my sister quickly became best friends. Eventually he married my oldest sister, Jean.

Our families blended and began sharing among each other. Francis' family is from Louisiana. We got to learn about and experience a different culture. That included delicious food like gumbo and boudain,

I always thought that Francis and my sister made a

perfect couple because they were smart, caring, and kind. Francis has a wonderful demeanor and a big heart for God and people.

He'd give anyone the shirt off his back if they needed it. I have never seen anything that would suggest he had the ability to be mean, yell, or scream.

Francis is always quick to recognize my accomplishments. He has done this since the beginning.

While in the Army, he served our country in the Vietnam war as a Specialist 5 Mechanic. This rank qualified him to work on Army helicopters and any of the other Army flying transportation which was used. He could repair anything that the Army flew.

While away from his family he looked forward to the care packages we regularly sent. We wanted him to have a touch of home while serving.

He said that his fellow comrades were just as excited as he was when his packages were delivered. They knew his family always sent something delicious such as his mother-in-law's molasses tea cakes. They looked forward to Francis sharing.

After many years of serving, Francis returned to the United States. We were delighted because God watched over him and brought him home safe.

He continued in his role as my big brother. Charles was in college at the time, and my oldest brother, Jesse was a truck driver who was on the road a lot. Francis stepped up and filled in.

He seemed to always there when I needed a big brother the most. He assisted me with my homework, and general counsel.

For example, he was there to ensure I attended and returned to events, dances, and other gatherings, safely.

My mother did not drive, so after work, he went home and made sure my sister and their children were situated, and then he came to our house and ate dinner with my mother and me before driving me to my very first sock-hop when I was in seventh grade.

He encouraged me not to rush after the dance. He wanted me to enjoy my friends before I was picked up shortly after nine o'clock that evening.

Then, he returned to my mother's house because my mom would always bake a chocolate cream pie for him. The two of them would then sit down and watch television as they enjoyed dessert.

Later, I came to realize that my brother-in-law enjoyed learning from my mom. She would always pray for, talk and laugh with him.

Francis went back to school and earned his college degree and became an architect. He received an associate degree from Fresno City Junior College.

Then he transferred to California State University, Fresno where he graduated with an architecture and engineering degree.

Francis had talent in these areas of studies long before he went to college. In his senior year of high school, he designed the large monument presently standing at Edison High School in Fresno, California.

After finishing school, Francis accepted a job as Principal Engineer for the County of Fresno. At this post, he developed an innovative landfill recycling program which was used throughout the State of California.

He also introduced a recycling program and other environment-friendly programs to the county of Fresno when no recycling program existed.

Before he retired, he was also named Engineer of the Year for the state of California.

Today, Francis spends his time in service with his church and taking care of his family.

We celebrate along with other family members when there are birthdays, holidays, Super Bowls, and any event where there is cause for celebration.

I will always be grateful for how Francis stepped in during a crucial time of my life.

The old adage, *it takes a village,* absolutely was applicable to our family. Suffice to say, neither nannies nor au pairs were in the budget, nor were they necessary as my siblings and I grew up.

Although we remain a very close family, we are not a perfect family. We have our bouts and moments; and there were times when we didn't like each other very much. Nevertheless, and in four words; *my siblings are sensational.*

My family had always seen me as a strong woman. It was rather difficult for them to accept that a soft-shell tick infection had debilitated my body.

I could see in their faces that they were struggling to adapt to decreasing levels in my mobility, agility, and strength.

My humor, energy, and joy were still a part of me. Still, in their hearts, I wasn't the sister and 'Aunt Sheila' they had known for decades.

My nephew wrote and dedicated the following poem to me. It's titled, *Resting In His Grace.* It reminds us both of our positions when we are greatly challenged.

Resting In His Grace

by Andrew Gordon

Here, I am with all my flaws,

In awe that you love me at all

Yet you lift, sustain, and keep me

Not seeing me as I am, but what I will be

You exchange guilt for grace,

You forgive me and all my mistakes

Perfecting me, giving me another chance

I thank you for your faithfulness

I praise you for your holiness

I rest in your grace as I seek your face

I find shelter and safety in that secret place

When disease and affliction reared its ugly head,

You told me that healing was the children's bread

By your stripes I am healed

You helped me to trust in you and believe

When I struggled with doubt and low, self-esteem

You reminded me that you loved me

That I could do all things through Christ who strengthens me

My life is filled with Divine favor

Blessed by the Almighty, Savior

Truly there is no one more powerful or greater

I rest in your grace,

You relieve me of my burdens and weights.

I find peace in your loving embrace

Not knowing what I do

It's You, I pursue

I wait on you, and my strength is renewed!

Help me daily to live right,

Live a Holy life in Your sight

You died, taking my place

My sins are now erased!

I am a new creation in Christ

I will serve you for the rest of my life

Grateful for undeserving Grace

You saved me from damnation and disgrace

Hallelujah! I'm energized by resting in Your grace

The Miracle Child

O *ne of the greatest of God's gifts is the ability to recognize His amazing handiwork. That's why it's important to keep your eyes open and listen for his voice. Always be on the lookout for his presence; you don't want to miss it.*

As I reflect over my life, I can't help but be awed by the many great things God did for me. With each passing year, I would experience even more.

Even though I didn't know it at the time, God was preparing me to recognize 'the why' behind countless life events. I recognize this as the purpose of my life. When one grasps why they are here along with others, then one begins to understand their life's purpose. There's no coincidence about coexistence. We all have a definitive, life purpose that almost always requires discovery.

What an amazing time it was to be alive!

I was one of the disc jockeys at Fresno State University Bulldog Radio for two semesters. As a journalism major, I enjoyed that very much. Interesting enough, even though I never realized my dream of being a cheerleader in high school, as a freshman at Fresno State University, I became a varsity cheerleader after trying out and making the squad. Eventually, I became the head cheerleader at F.S.U.

I remember the time that I finished taking early exams for the semester. It was preceded by hours of cramming because all of our work needed to be turned in before we left for the trip.

No exceptions.

Minutes into traveling with our basketball team for a tournament in Reno, Nevada, I realized that I wasn't feeling the greatest. I was curled up in a jacket and all I wanted to do was sleep. It was snowing I was feeling very nauseous.

My girlfriend and fellow cheerleader, Rona, felt my head.

"You don't feel like you have a fever."

Still, she was very concerned. She knew it was unlike me to be without a cheery disposition. I remembered I wanted to cry but didn't. I also remember going in and out of sleep.

At some point, the athletic trainer observed me and determined that I had a low-grade, fever. I was given two aspirins.

As we continued the six-hour, trip I became increasingly tired and sick. I was experiencing pain in my abdomen. I didn't know it then, but the pain was similar to that of appendicitis.

It involved a gradual onset of dull, cramping and aching pain that ran throughout my abdomen.

The pain level quickly escalated to absolutely unbearable. What was worse, every passing moment sharpened points of acute pain.

When the bus stopped for a meal break, I wasn't able to leave the bus. However, teammates, boosters, and fellow cheerleaders made sure that I had soup and food to eat

Unfortunately, I was unable to keep anything down.

After arriving at the hotel several hours later, I was completely incapacitated and unable to walk. My entire core was under attack and I was too weak to do the long walk to my room.

One of the basketball players carried me to my room.

Everyone came back and checked on me periodically to make sure that I was okay, but I wasn't doing very well. It seemed I was being antagonized by sharper and sharper pains.

My lower abdomen hurt so badly I could hardly walk. I tried my best to hang in there. I rationalized that if I did, I could join my squad and the team at the tournament in a day or so.

Deep in my heart, it really didn't seem possible.

I stayed in the room and took a warm bath. My hope was that immersion and warmth would ease my lower back and stomach.

It didn't.

I wanted my mama. I called her immediately and told her I needed to come home. For her to make that happen would require paying for a flight that we did not have the money for.

As I processed that reality, a female basketball booster knocked on my hotel room door. She wanted to check on me.

Sensing how ill I was, she immediately agreed that I should return home.

The coach had one of the boosters make

arrangements for me to fly home. My team helped me pack and I was taken to the airport.

When I arrived at the airport, I was transported in a wheelchair.

I was in excruciating pain as I sat waiting to depart. I cried continuously. Reminding myself that my sister was meeting me in Los Angeles seemed to make the pain, subside.

The flight from Reno, Nevada to Fresno, California felt like the longest hour I ever spent anywhere.

While on the aircraft, I alternated between crying silently, and sobbing incessantly.

The discomfort was horrendous. I wanted so badly to lie down and curl up in the fetal position, but that was not an option.

The stewardesses were so compassionate and did their best to make me comfortable.

When the plane landed, I discovered that I still could not eat anything that would stay in my stomach.

My sister met me in Los Angeles. Slowly and painfully, I went from the airport to her car. The two of us then drove to Fresno to meet our mother.

It was soothing to see Mom. She knew I needed

immediate, medical attention so we went directly to the hospital.

When I was admitted, the nurses took several blood samples. However, even though I was in extreme pain I was given nothing to alleviate it.

This was the most painful and frustrating, coming of age experiences, ever.

The next morning, a very young nurse or candy striper—I'm not sure which title she held--walked into my room. I had not seen her before. She asked me to sign a paper that gave the doctor permission to perform surgery.

My brain went, numb.

I thought the request was quite strange. It made very little sense, so I questioned the rationale.

"Why does the doctor want to operate on me if he doesn't really know what's wrong with me?"

She responded aggressively using scare tactics. Although her words were wicked, it didn't necessarily mean that she was wicked. I knew she was 'the messenger.'

"If you don't sign and get this done immediately, there could be some difficulties down the road," she said with a subtle arrogance.

What? I silently said to myself.

Was she trying to intimidate me into having surgery? It sure felt like it. A flash of anger crossed my vision. I wanted and *needed* my mom, badly.

She continued to speak.

"The doctor needs to operate to find out what is wrong. The only way they can do that is to do exploratory surgery. There is a remote possibility that he may have to remove your ovaries and uterus."

I repeated, *"What?"*

This time I asked out loud, I could not believe what I was hearing.

I could barely believe what I heard. My voice tightened with resentment. The remark had me stunned by bewilderment.

"Pump the brakes. I'm not signing anything and I'm not having surgery," I said belligerently. "I'm twenty years old and have never had children. If you do that, I will *never* have kids."

I then directed her to give me the phone. I needed to call my mother who had returned home to sleep. I dialed and waited for my Mom to pick up the phone.

"Mom, you need to get here immediately. They want me to sign papers to take my stuff!"

"What stuff?" asked my Mom.

"My stuff," I responded.

With the added emphasis, Mom knew what I meant.

"Don't sign anything; I am on my way."

My mom was very kind but became very stern when she believed her children were in harm's way.

"We'll just wait until my mother gets here," I told the nurse as I hung up the phone.

Crossing my arms, I repeated what I said earlier—this time in a mumble.

"I'm not signing anything."

The young lady knew I was alert and keen. She was not getting an okey-doke signature from me to take back to the doctor.

A few hours later another nurse with clip board entered my room. She told me I was being x-rayed, again. It would be the second time in one day.

At this point I was hysterical and asked why I was being x-rayed, again. I was perplexed. I hadn't been shown the results from the first one.

Additional blood samples were taken as well.

To add insult to injury, I still had not had anything to eat. An IV had been sustaining me, but I wanted to eat real food.

My mom arrived sooner than I expected. It felt so good to see her. She knew I had not eaten and brought food. However, the nurse didn't want her to feed me because the doctor wanted to perform exploratory surgery.

When the doctor greeted my Mother he made a statement that rocked my world. It completely caught me by surprised. Never did I ever imagine a doctor blatantly lying.

It was surreal.

He looked at my Mother and said, "We found that your daughter has a venereal disease which is causing her problems. It may have infected her ovaries and her uterus."

"This doesn't make sense," my mother replied is disbelief. "I talk with my daughter all the time. She's a virgin. How is this possible?"

The doctor appeared to be struggling with his

conscience and didn't respond immediately.

"Well you know," he said after a meditative pause, "We don't always know what our kids do or say. Your daughter has gonorrhea."

"That's not true!" I responded vehemently.

I could not believe what he said. He was lying, and I was livid. I immediately started crying.

Mom looked at me and sternly said, "Stop crying."

She believed me but wanted me to be strong in the face of my accuser.

Then, turning to the doctor, she asked how he was able to determine his diagnosis without her daughter being tested for gonorrhea.

He didn't have an answer for that.

I was furious.

Basically, he told my mother that I was lying about my virginity. Even though I was instructed not to, I cried, and I cried because this man of authority lied about my character. I did not know everything, but I knew better.

The American Medical Association has principles and standards. It involves a code of conduct and ethics.

He violated these.

I was concerned about my health and well-being. It was unfortunate that the doctor didn't share the same concern.

As a twenty-year-old woman, I wondered why he never said anything to me.

Then, it occurred to me that he was lying to justify the unnecessary operation.

But why?

His communications were nowhere near a moral compass. I didn't know it then, but I know now that having their reproductive organs removed was the fate of thousands of young ladies who were naïve enough to sign 'the form.'

That early evening, both the doctors and nurses were going through the motions. We still had not seen the results of the x-rays, nor were they ever discussed.

His actions and words led us to believe that the medical team was planning to do something.

My Mom and I decided there would be no surgery. She knew something was not right and requested more information.

I don't think he or his staff liked that. We didn't see

them for a while after that.

My Mom decided to call our minister for support. After a brief conversation, he told us he and his wife were on their way.

I was raised in a church that believed in laying on hands, and praying for the sick while believing for God's healing power.

As I was lying in my hospital bed, I asked Jesus to please help me; and help the doctor retract the lies that he spoke against my character.

I also prayed that the doctor return with a diagnosis that we could understand so we could make a sound decision about was going on with my health.

It wasn't long before our church bishop and his wife arrived. The sight of both of them was comforting. My bishop told me not to worry because the Lord will heal me in three days.

After assuring me, he and his wife privately spoke with my mother.

Then, the three prayed for me and laid hands on me. Three hours later, I realized that the pain began to subside. The bishop told my mother that I would not need surgery, and I did not have a venereal disease.

He went on to say that we should absolutely not allow the doctor to perform any operation because that particular hospital was known for performing excessive and controlled, birth procedures on young, African American girls, and other women of color.

Needless to say, I decided that I would not be added to that group or its statistics.

My mother then requested food for me because there would be no surgery.

I left the hospital three days after I was admitted. The pain stopped and I have never experienced any pain in the area since then.

There is no doubt in my heart that Jesus heard our prayers and healed me. He saved me from being taken advantage of through a system that does not care about others.

Years later, when I was married, my husband and I were trying to have children; I had a procedure done to see to see if my tubes were blocked. After that procedure, the doctor made a statement that completely caught me off guard.

"I thought you said you never had surgery," he stated, somewhat perplexed.

I was stunned by his statement.

"I haven't. I came close; but I never did."

The doctor paused before saying, "Well, I just want to let you know that you have the most interesting scar on your appendix. It looks like someone has sewn it up. By the way, it's nice work. It looks really good."

Only God could have operated on me and sew up my appendix like no mortal doctor ever could. This confirmed why the tumultuous pain in my abdomen for more than thirty-six hours, suddenly stopped.

When I left my doctor's office and I got in my car, I sat there and asked Jesus a question I already knew the answer to.

"Jesus, did you sew my appendix and save my life fifteen years ago? Yes, you did! Thank you."

I had a ruptured appendix which could have been fatal. The hospital either did not catch it, or chose not to address it; so, Jesus stepped in.

He healed my appendix by sewing up the rupture without external evidence of me ever being cut open. I knew He had reserved my life for a greater purpose.

Knowing that God loved me enough to save my life by performing a supernatural surgery had me crying like a baby.

This was one of the many times that God showed His power, grace, and mercy. He saved my life by snatching it back from death. His power, grace, and mercy are sufficient.

Appendicitis is a medical emergency that almost always requires prompt surgery to remove the appendix. Left untreated, an inflamed appendix will eventually burst and spill infectious materials into the abdominal cavity.

This can lead to peritonitis, a serious inflammation of the abdominal cavity's lining (the peritoneum) and can be fatal unless it is treated quickly with strong antibiotics.

Sterilization, African American Women and Other Women of Color

What if you went to the hospital for a common surgical procedure such as an appendectomy, but the appendectomy was never performed. Instead, the focus was to manipulate and misinform you to the point where you were sterilized for no medical or justifiable reason.

As an adult, four decades after the appendectomy that was not performed by any medical doctor, my research has shown me that the attempt to sterilize me by removing my reproductive system was not an isolated incident. There was a reason for it.

Women of color were targets of sterilization. Most were falsely diagnosed as promiscuous or feebleminded. Those women who were actually sterilized reportedly suffered greatly.

Many marriages ended in divorce and the development of mental health problems ensued.

During the 20th century, innumerable teens and women of color were admitted to hospitals for routine procedures and minor and surgical procedures and were sterilized without their permission.

This act is known as medical racism and was ramped among African Americans, Native Americans, and Puerto Rican women report being sterilized without their consent even after giving birth.

Others say they unknowingly signed documentation allowing them to be sterilized or were coerced into doing so. The experiences of these women strained relations between people of color and healthcare personnel.

Countless numbers of Americans who were poor, mentally ill, from minority backgrounds or otherwise regarded as "undesirable" were sterilized as the eugenics movement gained momentum in the United States.

Eugenicists believed that measures should be taken to prevent "undesirables" from reproducing so that problems such as poverty and substance abuse would be eliminated in future generations.

By the 1960s, tens of thousands of Americans were sterilized in state run eugenics programs, according to NBC News. North Carolina was one of 31 states to adopt such a program.

Between 1929 and 1974 in North Carolina, 7,600 people were sterilized. Eighty-five percent of those sterilized were women and girls, while 40 percent were minorities (most of whom were black).

The eugenics program was eliminated in 1977 but legislation permitting involuntary sterilization of residents remained on the books until 2003.

Unfortunately, this was all-too, common protocol occurrence during the 1960s and 1970s.

My source is Nadra Kareem Nittle. She has written about education, race, and cultural issues for a variety of publications including the Robert C. Maynard Institute for Journalism Education and Change.org.

Sheila Anthony-Shaw

The Pageant World

The first pageant that I ever entered was in 1978. It was a county-wide, open call for beauty pageant contestants. It came with the opportunity to become Miss Black Fresno.

I use the term, "Pageant World" for a few reasons. Beauty pageants sit in a stratosphere all by themselves. They have their own solar system and the stars are part of the elite class.

My biggest incentive for entering was when I discovered that if I was crowned the winner, I would receive a $1,500 scholarship for my college tuition and books. That was as exciting as it was needed.

I knew very little about the beauty pageant world. I did know that there was a swimsuit competition and the contestants wore swimsuits, evening gowns, and they paraded around the judges.

Women of color were banned from entering early beauty pageants and participating along with the "white race."

This racial divide was rarely spoken about by anyone.

After 1940, the ban was dropped. That only meant women of color could enter, but they were neither wanted nor accepted.

African American women were told in advance, "You can enter if you'd like; but you're not going to win."

This is the impetus behind Miss Black America and other pageants such as Miss Black Fresno. And, it was one of the reasons why I entered.

The Miss Black Fresno pageant compensates for the lack of beauty competitions which warmly accept Black contestants. It is a platform where each contestant's beauty and intelligence could be displayed and recognized.

When I entered, I did so not understand what was expected from me. There were no instructions, playbook, or anything that would prepare me. However, it was apparent that these resources were available for a select few of the other contestants.

I could tell who was favored and saw how only a few were being coached to win. Nevertheless, I went along with the program and learned as much as I possibly could.

I recall rehearsing for hours wearing my top hat and shoes as I danced and sang to Michael Jackson's, *You Can't Win.* I didn't perceive it as being a negative song.

The lyrics talk about the race of life and how one runs to get to their destination, but there are times when you feel like you're being intentionally stopped before you reach the finish line.

However, the judges and trainers did not see it that way. At the end of the pageant, I was told by the judges that the reason that I did not make the 'Top 5' or even the 'Top 10' was because I was a very negative person.

The choice of words was harsh and caught me completely off guard. I was shocked when I heard their rationale.

My eyebrows rose as I silently asked, *"Really?* That's what you consider to be negative?"

To further add to my disappointment, I was not—but should have been advised to choose another song in advance of the dozens of hours I rehearsed my performance.

I eventually shook the hurt off and began to seek other pageants near Fresno that had open calls for contestants.

My second venture into the beauty pageant world led

me to enter the "Miss Fresno County," competition. It was serendipitous.

One day, my two girlfriends and I were sitting in the student union at Fresno State University. As we read the college newspaper, we came across an ad for a beauty contest that piqued our curiosity.

I wanted to enter for two reasons. One, the $1,500 scholastic scholarship was an exciting and much-needed, incentive. And two, African American girls were entering pageants. They simply were not wanted. I wanted to be part of change.

My girlfriends and I continue to discuss the pageant. What we least expected to do, suddenly sounded fantastic.

Even though the competition was a world that wouldn't warmly welcome us, it was a potential goldmine for three, broke college students. We were thrilled.

We discussed whether or not we would respond to the ad and answer the open call for beauty contestants. It didn't take us long to ask ourselves, *'Why not?'*

My girlfriends knew I had participated in pageants before. We decided to enter Miss Fresno County, together. We rationalized that we had nothing to lose, and everything to gain.

One of my girlfriends was an Opera singer, and another one was a dancer who specialized in floor routines.

I was planning to sing for my talent presentation.

Beyond excited, we gazed around the table at one another. I began to list the reasons we should enter.

"One; we're pretty—right?" Two; we have the swimsuit competition covered with our very athletic bodies. Agree? And three; we can walk in heels."

No one could argue with my points.

"Then, we're in! Oh, and don't forget that we're smart! The worst that could happen is that we don't get picked, and we don't win the money."

It wasn't long after we registered before the three of us were in the middle of rehearsals.

This was the thirty-five year pageant history that there were three, African Americans in the competition. It was fun and exciting to be a part of history.

The judges were looking for young ladies who took care of their health, bodies, and minds and had intellect. The winner would also have to demonstrate that she could serve as qualified ambassador for the pageant for a period of one year.

The winner of the "Miss Fresno County USA," goes on to compete in the "Miss California USA." Then, the winner of that competition is entered into the "Miss Universe," competition.

As a contestant, my dresses were all hand-made by my mother. And, I was able to dye a pair of white shoes and my white swimsuit from my first pageant pastel-peach to match one of my dresses and shoes for the second one.

The purpose of me entering the pageant was to win scholarship money, so it didn't make sense to spend money if I didn't have to.

It was not unusual for many of the contestants to spend hundreds and even thousands of dollars for dresses, shoes, and swimsuits. My family did not have that discretionary income, so I had to manage the little money I did have.

I met a lady who was an expert in the pageant world. She had appeared as a contestant in pageants, herself, and had intricate knowledge and insider secrets that she freely shared. It was clear that this was her life's devotion.

For example, she introduced me to the brands of lotion to use on my legs that did not cause the skin to shine as many lotions do to this day. I was also educated on the type of makeup to wear.

It was my first introduction to products that didn't leave a shiny appearance on the skin; as well as brands and techniques which brought out the best features from a distance.

Unlike the first pageant, I was given a playbook. I was thankful for that. It taught me how to find my best colors, shoes for my height, swimsuit, and of the like. It was an interesting process and it was where I learned about the pageant world.

What I discovered is that pageants are in a world all by themselves. Men and women are heavily vested in the scholarships, sponsorships, publicity, and community relations. The pageant world has its own economy.

I had a wonderful time meeting new people and learning new things. During rehearsals, we were instructed to walk, sing, and dance. As we did, we were picked apart like a plucked chicken.

The coaches and coordinators were masters in finding the smallest of flaws and deflating self-esteem flatter than any tire.

The three of us were constantly reminded that we were not going to place because the judges will never pick a black girl. One contestant laughed sarcastically as she told me I wouldn't win but I *might* get "Miss Congeniality."

During the four months of rehearsals for the Ms. Fresno County pageant, I was told several times by participants and organizers that a black girl would never be crowned.

I had no bitter feelings even though we entered a world where we were not wanted.

I will see every opposition as an opportunity.

– Sheila Anthony Shaw

The comments from the contestants who preferred that we not be there didn't discourage me. And, it mattered not that the participants and organizers were not open to inclusion and diversity, I was determined to get the judges attention.

After months of preparation and rehearsals, the pageant happened. The contestants were judged in front of a crowd of nearly one thousand people in a building that sat five hundred.

The judges critiqued the performances during the interview, talent, fitness, evening wear, and stage questions. After compiling points and notes, a decision was made.

Wow.

Adding to the unprecedented event were my girlfriends, whom   I encouraged to enter the pageant with me. Victoria H. Jones and Jacqueline K. Smith were crowned second runner up and third runner up, respectively.

I was crowned Miss Fresno County 1980, by Vicki Walker, Miss Fresno County 1979; and Deanna Rae Fogerty, Miss California 1979-1980.

Despite the passive-aggressive taunting, we never considered dropping out of the pageant. We had gone too far. Eventually, the three of us impressed the judges just enough to win.

The three of us had just done the unexpected. It was unprecedented. We were beyond thrilled.

The African American community in Fresno, California was overjoyed. I suppose other communities around the world who knew were also.

We shook things up, and I don't think many people were ready for that.

It occurred to us that there was a lot more to this than just entering a beauty pageant. It was a life lesson in grace, etiquette, and learning about your inner self, under pressure. This is what reflects real beauty.

This life lesson taught me that building self-esteem and confidence in the midst of adversity could transform one for the better. It made me aware that God was smoothing out the rough edges of my life. It also taught me that beauty was never meant to be manipulated or exploited.

I learned to work with others without being self-absorbed. Most importantly, I gained an understanding of who God had made me to be--flaws and all. The adventure taught me that there's so much to learn in the areas in our lives which we deem okay, or right.

There will always be room for personal development and opportunities to work on positive thinking, rather than negative thinking.

I recognize this as the same process as when I learn the word of God. God helps us understand when He uses positive words when speaking to His children. As the result, His children can handle any situation, and never miss a beat when faced with adversity.

Choosing to enter the pageant was God's way to use me to bring light to others. It was an opportunity to communicate in a positive way, rather than react in a negative way.

Despite all the nitpicking and depleting banter, I had a fabulous time. I learned a lot of things, made new friends, and grew leaps and bounds spiritually, emotionally, and physically.

I left that pageant knowing that I could do anything that I set my mind to. I also learned that God had a way of working in me and through me to bring out the best and to draw others in.

It wasn't long before I realized that becoming the first African American to win the Miss Fresno County Pageant, in California, was more complicated than it should have been.

Unlike the Miss Fresno County pageant queens before me, I was invited to just one event to represent during my reign.

I did not receive a calendar for my public service duties and community events; nor did I have a schedule of ribbon-cutting appearances. In fact, there was very little communication from the pageant board.

Surprisingly, I was not offered any sponsorship opportunities. In no way was I supported or directed to represent the county as pageant royalty and service. Very little of all that was stipulated in the Miss Fresno County contract was executed.

Absent were the photo opportunities and community engagements that previous Miss Fresno County pageant queens experienced.

Unlike previous pageant winners, I was notified of only one appearance during my entire reign. This was the sum of my recognition and exposure.

My only public representation as Miss Fresno County, 1980, was in an extremely remote and sparsely populated area of the county. *Pepsi* was the title sponsor of my float appearance during the Loggers event held in North Folk, California.

It had to be difficult for city and county officials to accept, let alone, embrace the first, black Miss Fresno County. If not, it certainly appeared evident.

Also, my picture was not hung in the Fresno, California, City Hall along with previous winners of the pageant. It would take a protest by black leaders in my community, and three years after my crowing before it was finally hung along with previous pageant queens.

To add insult to injury, it was removed and returned to me a short time later

During my reign, the traditional year of public service by Ms. Fresno County was shortened by three months. The event organizers rationalized that time was needed to prep for the next pageant.

The day I was crowned "Miss Fresno County, 1980," the sun broke through, mightily. Then, without forecast, ever-present, gray clouds suddenly took over the clouds. The paradox was unfathomable.

The lack of events and recognition had my mind scattering. I thought, *if this is what it is to be "Miss Fresno County, I don't even want to enter Miss California.*

However, what hurt more than anything else, was not being invited to the traditional relinquishing of the Miss Fresno County title. I was denied the opportunity to crown my replacement. It was devastating.

As reigning queen, I was supposed to crown my successor; the 1981, Miss Fresno County.

That never happened.

I was not even invited to the 1981 pageant. Instead, a representative from the pageant crowned the new queen.

It's difficult to deny that the decisions made during my reign were not discriminatory practices. More actions gave credence.

After being crowned in 1980, I wasn't acknowledged by the pageant committee again until 1983. That was when the reigning, Miss America, Vanessa Williams, visited the pageant as part of her own title duties. I was invited to meet and have dinner with her.

At the time of this publication, pageant organizers for Miss Fresno County have not fully addressed my concerns or questions as a former title holder. They have also chosen not to respond to communications from my representatives.

I decided to choose Black History Month, 2019, to shed light and seek resolution on my plight. I used a press release as my platform.

My story told using a press release, can be found on Google by clicking on the "News" tab. It's titled, *Miss Fresno County 1980, Sheila Anthony, Seeks Resolution After Historical, California Event.*

The Real World

There was a time when money was tight, but I had to redirect my focus to complete school. The day came where I had to make a decision. I was torn between finding a way to stay in school and working full time.

What added to my quandary was that, due to budgetary restraints, Fresno State was cutting the classes needed for my degree.

I was just eleven units shy of graduating. This fact was an issue that I have struggled with for decades. Today, I know that I am no less of a person because I did not get a state or Ivy League school, college degree. The only thing that matters is that I did the work and earned good grades.

God can use you for His purpose. It doesn't matter what your formal education status is. He will finish the good work he has started in you. His plan for your life cannot be thwarted. Life lessons will be presented to all of us over the course of our lives.

While still in college, I began to focus on a vocation for my life. I entered the field of banking and worked my way up to management. I was a financial sales officer for Bank of America.

While being promoted within the industry, I made successful and conscious efforts to diversify environments that were in need of diversity.

My strategy was to do so as peacefully as possible. This was one of the many strategies that my mom taught her children.

Even as I did, I received more than a few direct, subtle, intentional, and unintentional racial remarks.

They came from strangers, friends, coworkers, management, and customers. Some were down-right, hostile.

Not once did I let any of them steal my peace or break my spirit. I attribute this to what my mother instilled in me for decades. I was able to tolerate people who were unable to tolerate people of color.

I am most appreciative that I did not experience any discriminatory treatment in terms of my aptitude and abilities by upper management. Otherwise, I would have never been promoted.

My First Love:
The Ultimate Betrayal

My first boyfriend was sophomore in college when we met at a 7-Eleven. He was handsome, had blue eyes. His charm and good looks swept me off my feet.

We enjoyed a light, fun, conversation. We decided to date and did so for two years before getting married. I wanted to be sure.

He was the love of my life and my first long-term, boyfriend. His appearance, voice, and mannerisms made him very attractive.

He humbly knew that. We enjoyed each other. We were both runners, although I was through after two miles, he continued on for three more.

We married in my church in June 1982. It was one of the happiest days of my life. My brother Charles walked me down the aisle.

My husband was in excellent physical condition and took pride in his body and possessions.

He was also a double black belt in Karate. The two of us made a point to jog, exercise, and eat healthy. We were a young, happy, and healthy married couple.

Shortly after I married, I was promoted to bank manager for Bank of America. I was the first in the history of the community. I not only worked hard to earn it, I loved it.

My husband was accepted to and completed the police academy. Immediately, he became a S.W.A.T. officer. This was highly unusual for a new graduate and speaks to his physical abilities and professional skill set.

As many realize, the life of a police officer as well as the life of a wife or partner of a police officer, can be incredibly stressful. The possibility of not returning home is always there.

To address these and other issues, the Fresno Police department invited the spouses and partners to a support group orientation to address coping strategies for this very purpose.

I attended and was absolutely shocked by one of the modules presented.

"Be aware: as long as your husband, wife, or significant other is part of the force, both of you will have to deal with the 'Three B's: bills, booze, and broads. They are inevitable."

That didn't sit well with me at all. After I processed through my shock, I raised my hand and politely asked the speaker to expound upon what he said.

The facilitator was not able to do so. He appeared to dance around the question. When he did say something that was on the subject, it was not comprehensive.

Where were the ethics in the life of a police officer? And who *is* responsible for upholding them?

Those were my questions.

The biggest reason that I challenged the speaker is because in my mind, he was planting a negative seed that was intended for the spouses and significant others of the officers to tolerate any unacceptable behavior made by the officer.

I could not speak for the other attendees that night, but I could speak on behalf of my husband.

He was not a heavy drinker. Nor was he financially irresponsible. It only took us eight years to buy our home.

I paused and reflected upon my mother's words. She taught her children to be patient and comfortable with individuals who do not look or think like us.

It wasn't long before I realized that I had slipped.

That experience at the meeting was a wake-up call for the department's philosophy and level of tolerance.

My husband and I could talk for hours about our future, and I loved the way I felt when we did. We wanted children and for eight years, we valiantly made an effort.

We spent a small fortune on specialists and prescriptions—including a thermometer that cost one hundred dollars.

It was difficult for me to see how easy it was for my sisters to get pregnant. When they did, it was always another month to be reminded that I was *not.*

None of this stopped us from enjoying life and each other as we did all the things happily, married couples did. We danced, traveled world-wide, and attended church.

Still, want we both wanted badly was a baby, and that was not happening.

I prayed constantly and never questioned God.

For the first ten years of our marriage, the biggest challenge was my in-laws. Specifically, the snide remarks they made towards and about me.

I just wanted their respect. It wasn't necessary to love me although that would have been nice. Being kind would have been appreciated.

Both of our families knew we were planning to have children. It was important to us that our children have a loving and respectable extended family. We tried for a decade to conceive, but to no avail.

Then, the day came that we were pregnant!

I was thirty-five. We both were thrilled beyond measure. I told everyone. In the early weeks my doctor ordered a series of tests. The embryo was not moving through my tube as expected and he was concerned.

He told me, "You have an ectopic pregnancy."

Although I did not have full knowledge of the term, I knew that it wasn't the best news

He went on to explain that an ectopic pregnancy could possibly advance to a ruptured, ectopic pregnancy. If that were to happen, it would become an extreme medical emergency in which a fertilized egg implants itself outside the uterus.

I had to be treated to avoid risks and complications that could have been life-threatening. Typically, an ectopic pregnancy is situated in one of the fallopian tubes. This was the case for me.

If I would have taken an ill-advised, risk to do nothing in hopes that the egg would grow.

Furthermore, it would be selfish, unwise, and potentially suicidal on my part. That's because the egg in an ectopic pregnancy is not able to develop into a healthy baby.

My doctor recommended emergency surgery. He explained that if the embryo was to continue to remain at that location, but continue to grow, my tube could rupture and cause internal bleeding and probable death.

Even though my life was spared once again, I couldn't help but feel embarrassed about announcing that I was no longer pregnant.

In retrospect, I now know that sounds silly. I had nothing to be embarrassed about. It was a tragic event, and God knew best.

"You can always try again," my doctor said trying to encourage me.

That was easy for him to say.

Shortly after our ectopic pregnancy, my husband called me to say that he was in a bit of trouble.

He explained that a girl walked into the police department and told his superiors that the two of them had been sexually intimate from the time she was 15 years old, until that day.

"What? I asked in total disbelief. "We're in the middle of trying to get pregnant?"

That would be the last conversation on our efforts to have a baby together.

That's because on that day, a young lady and her mother did walk into the police station and reported an affair which she was having with my husband.

It was the truth. Their affair began three years ago. She had recently turned eighteen-years-old.

The news was surreal. There was no way that I could have processed it fully with the myriad of emotions tearing at my soul.

How did I miss three years of all of the signs of his infidelity?

More importantly, what would ever lead him to molest a 15-year-old girl?

He was an officer in excellent standing and took pride

in his work.

The woman was a minor at the start of their relationship. That was enough for an immediate investigation. My husband did not deny his involvement and was terminated a short time, later.

I asked him, "Why now?"

He told me the girl made a bold move. He promised her that when she turned eighteen, he would leave me, but he never did.

Filing a report was the ultimate revenge.

As he continued to speak, he revealed that I first encountered the young lady when she approached me during one of his police officer's events.

"I'm really sorry that you lost your baby," she said.

That was odd, I thought.

Not only did I *not* know this young lady, I wasn't even informally introduced to her by anyone—not even her.

I deduced that my husband not only shared such sensitive information, he invited her to the event.

After he was terminated, my husband began to speak freely about their relationship. I learned that he met the young lady at her high school. He was assigned as a law enforcement liaison there. She was fifteen years old at the time.

At this juncture in my life, I seemed that I was constantly dodging something that was being hurled at me all the time.

Atrocities and trials were coming at me so fast, there were moments when I wasn't sure if I would survive or not. This was real life; I wasn't reading about it, hearing about it, or watching it on television.

This was happening to us. This was happening to me. I was overwhelmed, insulted, betrayed.

I felt unloved by someone who I thought would always love me. How could he do this to us?

Why did he do this to us?

It was humiliating and emotionally tormenting. He violated our vows and made a mockery of our loyalty and mutual respect. This was the ultimate betrayal—in the worst kind of way. I was devastated.

It almost goes without saying-being betrayed by the love of your life is a tumultuous, painful process.

His philandering shattered my heart; but I knew God was already going to work and healing my heart.

I put a lot of things on the back burner. I needed to

think and plan. Delving further, things began to make sense.

A little more than a decade into what I believed was marital bliss, my husband had told me that he didn't want to be married anymore.

Despite what he shared earlier I still was not prepared for it. I never imagined this scenario would be a part of our lives. I felt like a confetti popper that suddenly and loudly goes off. The little pieces that once represented the whole were now scattered on the ground.

If we had major problems that would lead him to commit adultery, he never shared them with me. I wanted to know what had diminished and disappeared, and when.

"What is going on?" I asked.

Although my husband was not cold in his response, he was barely communicative. He was contemplative, but not forth telling. He appeared to think through every word before speaking it.

"I don't want to be married anymore. I need to find myself," he said.

To his vague response, I replied, *"What do you mean you need to find yourself?"*

I wouldn't come to terms with his first statement. I pretended not to hear it to deflect the hurt. But I did hear it. He said he didn't want to be married to me anymore.

"I just don't want to be married anymore," he repeated. This time his response projected both agitation and uneasiness.

He spoke in circles never answering my questions, but he did continue to repeat that he did not want to be married anymore.

Okay. I heard you the first time.

I was shocked, deflated, and did not take time to process any of these events, fully. Still, I told him that I would accommodate his request.

It's one thing to be unfaithful, but your character lowers yet another level when you have sexual relations with a child.

It's despicable.

My mind began spinning a multitude of thoughts. I was prepared for everything in our marriage except this.

"The other woman" was first, his teenage mistress.

What was he thinking?

Did I marry a pedophile? Or did he evolve into one?

I needed emotional and legal support. I called my mother knowing that I could count on her compassionate, calm—but steely, demeanor.

I went to see her. I cried in comfort.

Just being in the presence of my mother provided the encouragement I needed to press on. She reassured me that if I persevered, I would get to the other side of this traumatic event.

What I loved about mom is that she never "bad-mouthed," anyone. She raised me so that my words, walk, clothes, and hair were all undeniably from a God-respecting, lady.

My Mom was not one to take sides. That wasn't her spirit. She loved my husband long after we divorced because she loved my husband before we were married.

That was my mom. She was just that special.

Strength and dignity precede overcoming. I knew there would be much to get through, but I also knew had the support of God, a loving family, friends, and my church to help me.

Collectively, the guidance and voices would serve as sources for my inspiration.

I knew that our forthcoming divorce would bring me a great deal of pain. He would experience his share as well. That was a given.

But I also knew it would birth a newfound independence. And, more importantly, it would bring me closer to God.

Ready for it or not, I would soon take a plunge into the back-story of our marriage. When I discovered that he had leased an apartment, I packed his things, put them in the garage, then I changed the locks to our home.

In the fall of 1996, my niece, Mia called me. She checked in with me and suggested that I think about spending some time in northern California with her.

It was a sweet gesture; and it wasn't a bad idea.

I could see myself relaxing the San Francisco bay area for a few weeks. Besides, I would have almost zero chances of running into the man that crushed my heart.

I contemplated making the northern migration to the San Francisco bay area and made the move. It was appealing. I needed a break. A change of scenery would be good for me. It would provide a great opportunity to clear my head before thinking about my next moves.

I continued to think things through. I had a great

network and, if I did decide to permanently relocate, I was confident that it wouldn't take long to begin another career.

The more I thought, the more I fell in love with the idea of living in a new environment. I was attracted by the multitude of possibilities.

If any of that was to take place, I still had to deal with complex array of exhausting tasks. When a married couple with joint assets suddenly part and go their separate ways, things can get extremely difficult.

Although I was thinking in terms of divorce, I knew from the experience of others that I would best protect myself and assets with an immediate and legal separation. I had already initiated that process and we were legally separated in 1995.

It didn't take me long to realize that even after the separation, I was still grieving and angry about my husband's infidelity. I didn't care for being in that mental state.

To this day, I wonder why he said he didn't want to be married anymore, but then refused to sign the divorce papers until two years later.

Uncertainty and opportunity are often paired together. God is with me wherever I go. The time had come for me to embrace that.

I Took My Heart to San Francisco

After much contemplation, I decided to accept Mia's invitation.

In the fall of 1997—September, to be exact—I left Fresno for the San Francisco bay area. Since I was only planning to visit for a few weeks, I only packed a few clothes.

The visit was wonderful. The change of environment helped tremendously. And, I enjoyed fellowshipping at my niece's church. That fed my soul.

Nowhere will you see such a beautiful and bold blend of ethnic cultures and opportunities. The Bay Area offered respite for scorching weather. One could always take a short trip to the water to cool off. It just seemed to be a great place to live.

Then, the inevitable happened.

I decided to make the bay area my new home.

For that to take place, I needed to come up with a plan.

I would stay with Mia until I secured a job. After that, I would look for and move into my own apartment.

A blessing of favor was granted. I had a new vocation and an apartment three weeks later.

When I initially moved to the bay area, I had order in my physical environment. My Rolodex was in full effect, and I enjoyed the company.

However, the moment I was alone, my thoughts raced through my mind, and then down my face. Each time I struggled with the thoughts of my husband, I found refuge by getting into my car and driving to the San Leandro Marina.

Once there, I stared into the distance. Had I looked I would have noticed how pretty the San Leandro Marina is.

Then, I wrote in my journal in tandem with my incessant flow of tears. I did this for three, consecutive weeks hoping to soothe my saddened and troubled heart.

My brain would flashback to Fresno; to the way things

were—and would never be again.

My marriage was barely challenged by any of life's events until out of nowhere, I was confronted with the catastrophic. The suddenness of it all was overwhelming. But I knew it would be in my best interest to move past the destructiveness for good.

Every experience should be a learning experience. There is always something to be learned and passed on. Pain should be optional.

In spite of how difficult it was to accept then, it could be an enlightening experience to share one day, I thought.

I knew the day would come that I could share what I learned, and how I grew with others.

The thing I had to remember is that I was not fundamentally flawed. Relationship misalignments happen. Finding fault in the other person is never the solution. Moving on with God was.

There I was, sitting in my car some twenty-one minutes from San Francisco, California. It's the city where people fly twenty-one hours to visit. It offered fantastic opportunities to forgive, as well as all the tools to prepare a new beginning.

Being hired in the telecommunications industry gave

me a much-needed lift. Things were developing and going according to plan: I would stay with my niece until I secured a job, then I would rent an apartment.

I had never lived on my own. I went from my mother's house to a home with my husband.

It didn't take me long to find an apartment. It was in the same complex my brother Charles lived in. I loved his apartment—everything about it. I decided I wanted to live there, too.

So, I did. With God's favor I filled out an application and was informed the apartment was mine just a few days later.

For some, moving is dreadful; but not me. I was thrilled to pack and move it. My niece, Mia helped me move into my one-bedroom apartment.

We laughed and joked as we unloaded boxes. At one point she asked me,

"Aunt Sheila, is something biting you?"

Apparently, the previous owners had pets, which would have been fine had I not been told that no animals had lived there. I was so distracted by the excitement of moving into my apartment, I had not noticed.

When I examined myself, it was clear that something

was biting me on my knees and my legs. Mia and I continued to be bitten by fleas as we continued to move in.

This was disheartening and somewhat annoying, but I consider the problem temporary. It had to be because I'm allergic to fleas.

After I informed the manager of the situation, an appointment was scheduled to steam clean the carpet. What I knew—but found hard to accept at the time—was that I had a major flea infestation.

My bed and all of my furniture were infected. This was a serious issue because I am allergic to fleas. When I got bit, the bite would blister to the size of a quarter.

What I didn't know was that steam cleaning flea-infested carpet provides a hosting environment for the reproduction of even more fleas.

Because the first round of cleaning was ineffective, more steam cleaning was ordered which only compounded the problem because it incubates the fleas.

The carpet should have been replaced, but it appeared that the manager of the apartment complex was trying to avoid that expense.

The infestation escalated to the point where the

manager was no longer willing to correct the problem. I had no other choice but to report it to the City of Fremont.

The City of Fremont referred me to Animal Pest Control who then instructed me on how to do ultrasonic sound pounding. The process dried out the fleas and carpet. After that, I used a super-duty vacuum to remove the residue.

That seemed to resolve the issue. It was unfortunate that this technique wasn't used earlier.

Falling for a Reason

The first time I fell in the bay area was awkward. I was walking on my way to a job interview when I suddenly lost control of my body and fell forward. I scraped my knee and tore my nylons in the process.

Prior to falling, I was aware that my left leg felt heavier—much heavier. It felt like I was dragging lead as I walked.

I remember thinking, s*o this is how the enemy wants to embarrass me.*

It didn't appear that anyone saw me. I got up on my own and went to the ladies' room. Then, I went to and enjoyed my interview.

I got the job!

I was happy, but not without a little concern. I began to fall more often and wondered what was going on with my body. I could never seem to break my fall because my muscles froze. However, I was able to get up.

Unfortunately, I would always fall on my face.

If I fall all the time, no one is going to want to keep me on, I thought.

At first, I was humiliated. Later, it didn't matter so much to me. I told myself, as long as I am conscious and breathing, I am okay.

I was single and enjoying a thriving career with Cellular One. My daily commute was from San Leandro, to Morgan Hill. The distance was about 27 miles and most of that included congested traffic.

I didn't mind. I loved my vocation and enjoyed reaping the rewards that my success brought. I reached 155% of my annual quota with Cellular One in three months. Things were going very well and I was soon promoted to assistant sales director.

I was opening my third, Cellular One store when during the grand opening, I fainted and went down face-first. Embarrassed but I hated that my mishap was taking away from the celebration.

I was determined that I would persevere and went on with having a normal life as much as I could.

I began dating and had the pleasure of dating one the Golden State Warriors. As such, I was his guest during many of the Warriors' home games. I won't mention the since-retired player's name.

In 1999, my life began to drastically change. There were moments when I would walk and my joints would suddenly stiffen and lock. I would lose my ability to balance myself and fall down—usually directly on my face.

These events happened in the mid-nineties. I was in my forties.

For I will restore health to you and I will heal you of your wounds, says Yahweh, because they have called you an outcast saying it is Zion, whom no man seeks after.

(Jeremiah 30:17, NIV)

My body was under attack. I had sought the medical care from dozens of doctors and specialists and not one of them knew why.

My joints continued to stiffen and stay stiff for longer periods of time. This rigor state rendered me vulnerable to my entire environment.

As such, I was never able to brace myself when I fell as my entire muscle group failed. The group on the left side actually froze.

When hitting the ground, I typically landed on my face. One time I landed on my left shoulder. That fall led to surgery to repair my rotator cuff.

I was losing my mobility and that is why I was having trouble walking. The question was, *why was I losing my mobility?*

I didn't know; nor did the doctors or specialists at UC Davis, UC San Francisco, and Stanford.

Nice to Meet You,

Bryan Shaw

B ryan Shaw and I first met online. I had never considered using AOL's matchmaking service. It was a platform for meeting and dating. Although it no longer exists today, it was responsible for budding millions of relationships.

I first discovered the service after my two nieces shared their successes using it. I had been single for seven years and was ready for a new beginning.

Both of them would go on to marry their romantic suitors. Today, more than twenty years later, they remain married.

My nieces tease me to this day about the first profile I posted. That's because my comments in the, "Share a little about yourself," section projected scowling and had hints of bitterness.

In retrospect, I am sure that was out of fear of being hurt again.

They laughed and asked if I was trying to scare the men away.

That was possible.

I began to consider that maybe my heart *wasn't* completely healed. I was communicating from an incredibly protective space at the time.

Bryan and I chatted online, did the email thing, and eventually spoke on the phone. He wanted to meet in person before I was ready. I didn't want to rush things and suggested that we go forward with a slower pace.

One thing was very clear, we both definitively expressed that we had expectations of getting married again. There was no interest in long-term, dating.

Anyway, almost a month went by before I agreed to meet him in person.

We met at a Starbuck's in Fremont, California, and hit it off quite well. As I recall, we spent at least four and a half hours there.

Whew.

It was nice to put an entire body to all those instant messages, emails, and voice.

Having chatted for hours, we realized it was time for a meal and after discussing several options, Olive

Garden, it was.

We both enjoyed continuing our conversation over a meal as much as our stomachs did.

I remember Bryan wanted to kiss me after our date. I politely declined. I never kissed anyone after the first date.

I wasn't offended.

Bryan was perplexed. I thanked him for our time together, said goodnight, and closed the door. Bryan would tell me later as he walked away, curled his hand, brought it to his mouth and then blew into his palm. He wondered if he had too much garlic with dinner.

I didn't think it was necessary to debate about not kissing on the first date. It absolutely is a personal choice.

I shared that I was influenced by my mother's teachings, as well as the teachings of Pastor Juanita Bynum. I am a disciplined student of bible-based, teaching. I readily and regularly apply the principles of what I have been taught.

I liked Bryan. And, despite our difference of opinion on first-date kissing, it was wonderful to see him in person. It was worth the wait.

He was humble, had a dry sense of humor, and a nice smile. He really seemed interested in what I was saying, and always prayed with me before we said goodnight.

We went on a second date, and several more after that. We continued to date even though my ailments continued to get worse.

Bryan began taking me to my doctors, physical therapy, and chiropractor appointments after I could no longer take myself.

When we first met, I was quick to tell him about my physical health. My central nervous system had started to compromise its functionality. I beginning to feel run-down, and found it difficult to walk.

It was painstaking to climb stairs, or any incline for that matter. I kept telling myself that I needed to work-out more. I did, and that only seemed to make things worse.

Unable to work without pain or the risk of falling, I went out on medical leave.

At the time, my body would randomly go through a rigid state. When this happened, I felt like a tin soldier. Without any warning, my muscles became inflexible and very stiff.

If I was standing or walking, I was subject to fall like

a tall tree that had just been axed. There were no triggers or warnings.

I told Bryan about the day I was at work and was not able to walk across the room.

He *still* wanted to date me.

Really?

Are you listening to what I'm telling you? I thought.

Because my mobility challenges had temporarily been compromised, I opted not to drive during three different times over the past thirteen years.

Pragmatically, it made sense to me. There's no doubt in my mind that my decision kept others and myself, safe.

I then told him about one of the most chilling days of my life. It was a living nightmare that occurred because of my condition.

During the incident, I was driving alone across the Oakland-San Francisco Bay Bridge.

Suddenly and inexplicably, I could no longer sustain the pressure my foot had been applying to the accelerator pedal.

As a matter of fact, I could not control my foot at all.

I began to panic.

My car began to quickly decelerate, and then drag. Cars behind me began to honk, fiercely. The drivers had no idea that I had lost control of my ability to maneuver my legs, let alone my right foot.

It was a nightmare in the middle of the day. My mind knew what I wanted it to do, but my body refused to comply.

My whole being became stiff, heavy, and rigid.

I panicked and wondered what was coming. It was surreal and had I allowed myself, I would have stayed in that state.

I did not allow myself to become overcome with anxiety. Instead, I began to immediately pray and go deep inside and fight with scripture. God is vastly superior.

God responded and brought me through the tunnel, and across the Bay Bridge. Had God not calmed me down, there is no doubt in my mind that things would have ended horrifically, differently. I give God all the glory. Neither I, nor any other drivers were hurt.

That incident was another reminder that as a Christian who has free-will, I have complete authority over my thoughts, decisions, and words.

Getting Serious

While dating Bryan, I was waiting for my disability status to formally process, I had exhausted all of my savings.

With no income or revenue of any kind, Bryan and I discussed becoming roommates. As Christians, we agreed we would be celibate and sleep in separate rooms.

Bryan lived in the beautiful Santa Cruz, mountains. The inspiring and breathtakingly landscape reminded me how mighty God is.

When Bryan worked, he put in long hours. I grew comfortable spending a lot of time by myself. I enjoyed a peaceful and quiet atmosphere that is non-existent in most of the bay area.

Santa Cruz is well-known for its friendly and laid-back, atmosphere. I like that.

Bryan's home also had stunning views and spacious

outdoor living space. I loved that. We were dozens of yards from the nearest neighbor. It was so serene—the perfect retreat from city living.

The wharf, beaches, the world-famous, Santa Cruz Boardwalk; along with the highly-acclaimed university, restaurants, galleries and shops just made it a great place to live.

When he returned home in the evenings, I enjoyed our conversations. We could talk about any subject for hours.

And, I was thankful to have a prayer partner—especially when my pain meds took a long time to kick in.

One day, I noticed that my pain was increasing in levels and episodes, and my circadian rhythm was off. I was disoriented and over-medicated and realized that I was sleeping most of the time.

I'd talk to God and discuss His promises. Then, I would call my mother. Calling my mother was a very important part of my day. Just hearing her voice brought me great comfort and joy.

So many times I would remind myself that this is a trial and God is shaping me. I know He is the potter and the wheel in my life.

I asked God, "What do you want me to do?"

He told me He was preparing me for a specific purpose. I was willing to rest in the wait. No matter how painful it was.

I Said, "Yes!"

B ryan and I were very compatible. I continued to enjoy his company and our conversations. Going out or staying in with him was a joy.

Within six months of dating, he proposed to me. I said, yes. We were extremely excited. That same day, we went to look for a ring.

We went to Zales' jewelry store in Pleasanton, California. At the counter, he asked to see quarter carat, lose diamonds. He examined it, then he asked to see a marquis. He like it and chose four, quarter-carat diamonds to put in the main setting in my ring.

My jaw dropped.

The jeweler saw my expression. She looked into my eyes and said, "Well sweetheart, as your love grows, so will the diamonds."

I thought that was cute.

I planned our entire wedding. Bryan was very

impressed. It was a small, intimate gathering of family and friends.

My husband is a man of God, and one of my blessings. Our story is incredible. God sent me to him. He walks in integrity; and his morals and values are impeccable.

God gave him a sense of humor which helped me through my fifteen-year journey.

At the time of this writing, we are celebrating seventeen years of marriage. God said:

"Whosoever findeth a wife findeth a good thing and obtains favor of the Lord." (Proverbs 18:22; NIV)

Bryan is divinely favored and loves me unconditionally; just as God loves me.

We were married on March 23, 2002.

During our fourth month as a married couple, my health took a turn for the worst. My bones, muscles, and just about every part of my anatomy hurt.

It was as unexpected as it was frustrating and painful.

I spiraled downwards with my illness. Everything— even the smallest of things—suddenly became extremely difficult, then impossible. I could not walk and had to use a wheelchair.

No longer was I able to shower without assistance. Walking down the hall became incredibly difficult. The pain was tumultuous and fired to all points of my body when I sat, laid down, or made the slightest move.

It even hurt to think.

It felt like something monstrous was unleashed inside me. I was at its mercy. I spent several hours each day sobbing uncontrollably.

I wanted to sleep and needed to sleep badly but couldn't. I scheduled another appointment with my doctor and saw him that same day.

When he asked me what level of pain I was at, on the scale of one to ten, I said, twenty-five.

The pain was literally off the chart.

That afternoon, I was incorrectly diagnosed with Ankylosing Spondylitis.

Ankylosing Spondylitis is a form of arthritis. The doctor gave me a prescription that was actually a shot. It was called **Enbrel** (etanercept).

Enbrel® is used to treat five chronic diseases, including moderate to severe rheumatoid arthritis. At the time, it cost $2,500 a dose.

Can you imagine?

I know; that's criminal.

I was advised to find a grant to continue my shot treatments. To my surprise, I applied and was awarded one. I was beyond excited and of course, grateful beyond measure.

However, after several doses it was clear that the shots were not working.

I neither was prepared nor expected that. One would think that expensive prescriptions were expensive for a reason—because they're effective.

It appeared that no matter what meds I took, the active ingredients stopped at the surface. They had no effect on the pain that was ferociously and mercilessly attacking my joints and my bones.

The time came to see another doctor. He diagnosed me with Stiff-Person Syndrome. That is actually the formal name.

Those who are challenged by Stiff-Person Syndrome have a spine that is beginning to fuse together. I was prescribed new medication which only made my symptoms get worse.

The conditions and the routine of seeing doctor after doctor were making me frustrated and apprehensive.

During this time, I was unable to get out of bed or even bathe myself. Bryan assisted me with these tasks and others. I recall Bryan reading the bible to me. The pain was so intense, I could barely hear him.

Perhaps what was most concerning about this diagnosis was that I didn't recall taking an MRI or x-ray that showed that my spine was beginning to fuse together.

My life was rapidly changing. I was approved for social security, disability, and Medicare. That was great news—at least, financially.

At this point, I knew the drugs were greatly affecting my mental faculties.

I was not the Sheila that I or my family once knew.

At times it seemed like just when I was consciously enjoying a break from the indescribable pain, it would once again descend upon me.

For more than three decades, I had always enjoyed speaking to God several times, daily. However, my disposition had become so debilitating; I couldn't even talk to God about it.

My brain struggled to make sense. I didn't know what day it was, and had difficulty concentrating. I was tired of seeing doctors who could not tell me what was going on with my body.

That wasn't the worst part.

The drugs were potent, brain depressants that pushed down the normal functionality like the spring in a pen is pushed down.

That's one of the reasons why I was sleeping so much. My brain was not producing the normal levels of neurotransmitters.

When I decided to stop taking these drugs, it was likened to releasing the resistance from a compressed spring in a pen.

Boing!

My brain launched a surge of adrenaline that kicked-off major withdrawal symptoms. I went from sleeping most of the day to insomnia and having difficulty falling and staying asleep.

That wasn't all. I experienced full-tilt, anxiety attacks; panic attacks; restlessness; irritability; muscle tension; racing heart, skipped beats, palpitations, fevers, and violent episodes of epileptic-type, spasms and seizures.

It was an extremely uncomfortable phase in my life; one that I never plan to revisit.

In total, more than fifty-five doctors and a handful of

infectious disease specialists could not tell me what was going on with my body.

My world as I once knew it was being altered as I once knew it. My heart grew heavy with despair, and suddenly, I wasn't producing enough red blood cells and my muscles went into an atrophy state.

The pain was so unbearable, I could no longer walk. The treatment and counsel that I was receiving from the doctors and specialists was not helping me at all. In truth, they were actually harming me.

I saw more doctors, took more tests, and received more medication. Nothing was conclusive.

Twelve years had gone by and I still had no clear-cut, definable diagnosis.

The pain continued to increase with each prescription added. It was unremitting, relentless, and tormenting.

Many of the doctors I saw—even if I only saw them once—told me that I would always be in a wheelchair.

They did not know the God I serve.

I felt abandoned by doctors and specialists. They seem to ignore or make light of what they were unable to diagnose. Only a handful—if that—mentioned the likelihood of addiction.

It would have been wonderful if I grew to be adept at controlling my pain with coping mechanisms. The pain was so excruciating, I simply did not have the wherewithal to do so.

Yea, though I walk through the valley of the shadow of death, I will fear no evil for Thou art with me. Thy rod and thy staff comfort me.

(Psalm 23:4, New International Version)

One neurologist wrote a prescription that raced my heart and mind. I was high on prescription drugs. I neither could calm myself let alone, be still.

I wanted it out of my bloodstream and with the help of Bryan, did my best to dilute the drug. I cleansed my blood as best as I knew how by drinking more than a gallon of water and walking.

Bryan had to help me walk. We walked in each room and every area of our house for more than eight hours from evening, until the next morning.

Sometime between 2005 and 2006, I was very much aware that I had transformed into an angry housewife. I was addicted to prescribed medication that I didn't even want to take.

Dr. Dawn Motyka saved me from myself. She was the one who help me identify the drugs that were not serving me. I was weaned off them, forever.

The Miracle and Dr. Wright

The day came where I saw my deep-tissue, massage therapist and we mostly talked and did very little physical therapy. That's because I was in so much discomfort, any type of contact was extremely painful contact.

She told me her son saw a specialist that helped him reach his medical milestones and she was confident that Dr. Wright could help me, too.

Dr. Wright is an infectious diseases specialist who is passionate about helping hurting people who are not receiving the proper treatment.

My massage therapist strongly advised that I contact him immediately. I was thrilled and already looking forward to meeting him.

Something in my heart told me that this doctor would be different because of how I discovered him. I believed that my massage therapist was chosen out of hundreds of choices for a massage therapist for such a time like this.

After I shared the news with Bryan we called and made an appointment with Dr. Wright.

In November of 2012, Bryan and I met Dr. Wright for the first time. I loved his demeanor and I knew he cared because he spent an hour and a half examining me, getting to know us, and my history.

Dr. Wright asked questions that no other doctor or specialist had asked before and during my examination.

I had a thorough, head-to-toe, examination. This encouraged me as none of the other medical doctors and specialists had done so.

One doctor in particular never came in the room. He consulted with me from the doorway. He thought I was contagious.

When the examination was over, I was directed to go to another facility for lab work, and I would meet with him again for his diagnosis.

That was comforting and assuring.

My next appointment was scheduled five weeks later; January of 2013. That single day in his office made my decade.

Before Bryan and I could be seated in his office, he

shared the results from the test, and his diagnosis.

He not only told me that he knew what was going on, but that it was treatable.

I was shocked—in absolutely the best kind of way.

My prayers were answered before he shared the details with Bryan and me. There was silent jubilation. It took more than a few seconds to fully take in what the doctor said, tears of joy trickled down my face.

Dr. Wright told me he knew what was going on with my body now. He knew what was wrong with me. And he knew how to treat me!

He knew!

I was filled with silent joy, tears streamed down Bryan's face. God was faithful.

Dr. Wright continued to share more about his findings and the treatment. As he spoke, I continued to tear. He was telling me what more than sixty doctors and specialists could not.

God bless his soul!

I had contracted a soft-shelled, tick-borne disease, relapsing fever and related illnesses. My guess is that it originated in the apartment I rented in Fremont. It's probable, but not conclusive.

Dr. Wright used a microscope to show me the spirochetes in my blood. It was the creepiest thing I have ever seen.

I had an infection which can only be passed on from tick to human or animal. It's not contagious and only transmittable by a tick carrying the disease.

He went on to explain that a complication developed from the tick-borne disease was causing brain to body, neurological miscommunications.

My prescription was forty-two consecutive days of antibiotics which would be administered through an IV. The consecutive days included Saturday and Sunday.

Precisely, the prescription is called intravenous antibiotic therapy and would be given to me Dr. Wright's office. Internationally, it's known as the Infusion Center.

For the prescription to be effective, I could not miss a day of treatment.

In order for that to happen, I had to be open to taking public transportation for the differently-abled and endure a two-hour, each way, commute. Bryan would take me on the weekends.

Seven to ten days of antibiotics in the form of a pill

was always followed by side effects such as stomach upset and queasiness.

I felt comfort knowing that my prescription was being given to me intravenously. My hope and prayer were that the side effects wouldn't sideline me.

Dr. Wright asked me if I wanted to start that same day. I emphatically replied, *"No!"*

Not because I was anticipating pain and wanted to delay it if I had an option. That was not the case.

Bryan and I were scheduled to participate in a marriage conference after the appointment with Dr. Wright that day. We were looking forward to the enrichment in Santa Cruz for that weekend.

Our church hosted the annual conference each January for married couples who desired to strengthen their marriage relationships. Lord knows ours needed the strength. We were in need and looking forward to the edification.

At the conference, I shared my testimonial with more than two hundred other believers. I explained that more that fifty-five doctors and specialists either were not able to, or misdiagnosed my illness. However, today before attending the marriage conference, a specialist told me exactly what was going on with my body.

I do believe that God waited for such a time as that so a large body of Christ could rejoice with me and Bryan. We all praised God for His faithfulness. It was wonderful! The victory was mine!

It was a momentous occasion filled with elation to share or testify to the glory of God.

Bryan and I shared the good news with family and loved ones. They all were excited, but I was *thrilled.*

When I got home, I went online and made the necessary phone calls to initiate my transportation to my appointments with Dr. Wright.

I was very excited as I went to work on coordinating public transportation from our home in Santa Cruz, to Dr. Wright's treatment center in Monterey.

I was in a wheelchair full time and would need special assistance while being transported.

Riding the bus was fine with me. I didn't have to be in my car—or anyone's car—to go out in the world.

After contacting several agencies from multitude counties and securing paratransit documentation, I was able to map out a plan with the different transportation providers.

Handy Ride transportation would pick me up at our

home in Santa Cruz. Then, I would enjoy a two-hour ride until I reached the Watsonville, California bus terminal. This was my transfer station.

Then, I would ride the Monterey County's disabled transit service, Lift Line. It would take me directly to Dr. Wright's office.

After my intravenous antibiotic therapy, I would be escorted to the curb where I waited for the bus to begin my reverse commute.

My commute and appointment took up a full day in my life. Once God showed me how blessed I was, I didn't mind the commute at all. It provided an opportunity for me to grow in patience.

I prepared snacks and brought crossword puzzles, books, and my teaching tapes.

I also packed large, *Ziploc* bags. In the past, high levels of antibiotics wreaked havoc on my body's systems. I experienced nausea, diarrhea, headaches, and vomiting.

There were days I had to alter the extent of the adventure. I was not going to be stopped. I was determined to see what I started through to the end.

I figured that if I anticipated an episode of vomiting, I could use my *Ziploc* bag for the fluid. I remain thankful to God that I only had two episodes.

In retrospect, I know that because Dr. Wright does not use serums or antibiotics with mercury in them, my body adapted to the antibiotics he used in the IV quite well.

The ride to my appointments offered a stunning view of the Pacific Ocean. Most of the drivers were very polite. I enjoyed the interaction I had along the way.

Interesting enough, each morning that I arrived at my transfer station in Watsonville, I would see the same four older Hispanic gentlemen sitting at the café next to the Watsonville bus terminal.

They sipped their coffees and casually checked their scratcher lottery tickets as they sat together. When we made eye-contact, they greeted me by smiling and tipping their hats.

Two of the four wore cowboy hats, and two wore baseball caps. I was both flattered and humbled by the gesture.

I didn't speak Spanish, so there was a language barrier. Nevertheless, they could see that being in a wheelchair who traveled alone daily on Lift Line, that I was presented with a challenge.

I saw their smiles and hat-tipping as a means of

encouraging me. When I smiled back, waved, and even giggled, I wondered if their wives kicked them out of the house each morning.

God raises up encouragers in our lives. If we are watching for His presence, we will encounter them. The gentlemen added to the joy in my day during my commute.

It took about two hours to get to Dr. Wright's office. My treatment took a little over an hour. When it was over, I made the return trip home to Santa Cruz via Watsonville.

During this time, I was especially blessed by one of my neighbors. She and her husband are always going out of her way to serve others. They graciously shared their fresh eggs, blackberries, and lemons with others.

One afternoon while talking on the phone with her, she offered to take me directly to my IV treatment on Tuesdays. I was greatly moved by the gesture.

After my appointment, the two of us would have lunch in Monterey and enjoy the ocean. I was very appreciative and enjoyed our conversation to, and from.

I received one gram of antibiotics each day via an IV. After about three weeks of treatment, Dr. Wright ordered more blood tests. The results revealed my infections were decreasing in intensity!

I was encouraged.

On the weekends when Bryan drove me to the treatment center, we always planned to do something fun afterwards.

At the end of forty-two consecutive days of IV treatment, I was given another blood test. The results showed *very* low levels of infection.

Dr. Wright was not concerned. I believe he expected these results.

However, Bryan's eyebrows rose with concern upon hearing the outcome.

"We're not done yet?" he asked. Dr. Wright. He knew the victory was ours, but he was clearly expecting, right-now, manifestation.

Dr. Wright looked at Bryan and smiled softly before saying, "Let's wait and see what happens."

Dr. Wright's response was blessed assurance for me.

I was elated. After four months of treatment, the blood tests indicated that I was completely free of the tick-borne relapsing fever infection. The WPA6-Whatever Infection was in remission, too.

We praised God.

And we continued to praise God.

We announced those results to our entire church in a church service one Sunday morning! There was great rejoicing and praising God's healing power!

Filled with elation, I shared and testified to the glory of God. It was yet another momentous occasion.

I claimed it, and I received it. God is faithful; and there is power in the name of Jesus. *God is so good.*

All of these events have proven to take place in God's perfect timing.

Unfortunately, due to the Centers for Disease Control recent decision, the life-saving antibiotics used in my IV are no longer available.

My hope is that Dr. Wright will be provided a platform in America where he can share ideas about infectious diseases and discuss treatments that have been proven to be effective.

It would be wonderful if the Centers for Disease control would be open to removing the medical bureaucracy so that the antibiotics which cured my infection can cure others.

The results from the treatment I received from Dr.

Wright were epic. His standard of care was above all of the more than fifty-five doctors and specialists who saw me.

My heart goes out to all whom—seemingly—will not have access to the healing treatment I had.

I thank God for my miracle. With Dr. Wright's assistance, I have completed a journey from a wheelchair and walker to a cane. He is an excellent educator who taught me things no other medical professional did.

For example, did you know that sour kraut boosts the immune system? He has used it in his treatments.

I take great comfort knowing that everything he shares and prescribes is backed by both research, and results. And, I am sure my massage therapist is not the only unsolicited ambassador for his work.

Looking back on how the thirteen-year journey impacted my marriage, I am thankful beyond measure that Bryan stood by me even when he was at his own wit's end.

My marriage and life were subject to being ravaged during this time in my life. By the grace of God, it did not.

For me, there is never a reason to reflect upon the

past, mournfully or resentfully when God is a part of your life.

My mom taught me decades ago that all attempts to take on the biggest unknowns without God, I would fail over and over again.

I spent years combating anxiety and frustration and on and on they went. Those years included sleepless nights, restless days, and obstacles.

I never gave up on who was inside me, or the promises He gave me.
Because of what my mother and an elder in my church reminded me of, I knew that each day of pain was bringing me closer to the solution.

I rested in God's grace. I knew that everything that was causing me discomfort was going to improve, and the turbulence would subside.

This reassurance always made me feel better. There was no reason to fear the unknown when you believe God will see you through.

Satan would rear his head more than a few times. Despite how I felt, I knew he was no match for the God I serve.

Whatever you are fighting against, struggling over, and going through, know that it is in your best interest because the manifestation of your healing—your peace—is on the way.

Although I was frustrated and exhausted, I did my best to remain hopeful and faithful. Without my faith and the loving and forgiving heart God blessed me with, this could have been a very bitter experience.

There is no regret when I think about what I could have accomplished had I been totally able and fully awake.

What matters is that God is faithful. He heard my cries and he answered me. Today, I no longer have a lingering illness and I am completely infection-free.

And, I can say despite the discomfort and confusion, I've grown to appreciate where I am now, and where I would like to go. Although I walk with a cane when I am out of the house, it's certainly not something that I have to depend on.

God stilled the waters in my life. I know He can do the same for you.

Mom Transitions

I was proud to share the life of my mother in the beginning of this book. With reverence and respect, I now share the events of her last days. This is my expression of gratitude and devotion. Each and every moment that we shared together was a gift.

Eula Mae Anthony was the one who encouraged me to keep God first if I wanted to reach the unreachable. She taught me to not to settle for anything less than I deserved.

I use this space because it is important to me that you know where my core values stem from...

The call was chilling. My sister told me our mom was in the hospital because she was having difficulty breathing. The hospital was the one place that my mother did not want to be an overnight guest.

Just three weeks earlier, Bryan and I had returned to the bay area from Austin, Texas. His father passed away. We jumped in the car and took the two-hour drive to Fresno.

It was wonderful to see my mom and I could see that she was happy to see us, too. Mom never cared for anyone coddling her. In her mind, it simply was not necessary.

I could see that her breathing was labored; but that was not her concern. She did *not* want to be in the hospital and asked that we drive her home.

We wanted to take her home but were told for that to happen, Mom needed a 24-hour, in-home caregiver. We made the decision to take her to a residential care facility.

We were advised by the hospital staff not to stay at home, long. Mom needed medical supervision and the equipment needed to make her comfortable and keep her alive.

Bryan and I drove her to her apartment and stayed there for a short period of time. She was appreciative, but she let us know that she wanted to pray in her own peaceful and quiet abode.

We fully understood and respected that. We left a short time later and readmitted her to the hospital.

Mom was also challenged by kidney problems and was on dialysis.

One day while Bryan and I were on our way to see her, we were told that dialysis was not working for her anymore.

On the day she transitioned, I received a phone call from the in-home, hospice nurse. She told me my mother was no longer breathing.

Eula Mae Anthony transitioned at the age of eighty-four. She looked every bit of being twenty years younger.

She remains deeply missed and ceremoniously, remembered.

My mother encouraged me all of her life. For that, I am thankful beyond measure.

Never forget what the Lord has done for you, go forward and share all you have learned with others.

- Eula Mae Anthony

The Day I Woke Up

I decided to take a break from driving. That meant I would have to take Handy Ride Para transit Services to get me to the meetings. The four-dollar fare was reasonable and affordable. I am ready to join my church's women's ministry and study the bible.

By accepting the challenge, I illustrated my commitment to the group that I yearned to be a part of.

On that morning in 2014, I was led to share with Bryan my longing to join the women's ministry at my church. I was very excited and he was very supportive. God had put the desire in my heart. I took it and worked towards it.

The irony is, I considered joining before but opted not to join the ministry after discovering how intense the 29-week training was.

The curriculum involved reading, studying, and demonstration of comprehension.

Had I known how much of a fun, loving, and supportive environment for learning was, I would have signed up much earlier.

There's a lesson there.

The ministry met weekly and still does. The group not only studies, but gains clarity on the teachings in the bible. It also inspires and prepares women to passionately pursue God while being an active light in this world.

After our meetings, we often go to a restaurant for coffee, dessert, or a meal. These gatherings further unite us and helped to connect us with others. We are indeed a sisterhood.

Perhaps the most enriching part of the fellowship is that we all share our collective wisdom and take due diligence in the application of God's word. We serve, lead and follow according to God's word.

The New Testament refers to women in the church as Godly women. Such was Phoebe. She was a minister and leader who worked with Paul. We strive to uphold that calling.

Three months into the study of Moses, I was asked to facilitate a group. I accepted and facilitated Beth Moore's teachings. As a part of the church, we lift, educate, serve to ensure it remains, whole.

I was honored. Teaching the material and using examples to illustrate and connect the concepts was fun. The joy of teaching resonates with my natural leadership style.

We are providers of tools, inspiration, support, and of course—the word of God. This contributes to a better life balance.

Among my biggest goals are to continue sharing the Word of God; and teach others how to rest in His grace.

Through his word, I aim to share my faith with those who desire a closer relationship with God. I dedicate my life so that the ministry that God gave me is sustained long after I leave this earth. My desire is to fulfill His will and purpose. I will continue to enhance the lives of all who God puts in my path.

If there was is one axiom to give you so you could best share the message with others, it would be: We all need words of encouragement and hope.

The beautiful thing is that when bible-based, training for men, women, and youth are part of a house of faith, and then these groups later come together, it strengthens the church as a whole.

The trainings and teachings have brought me to the present moment with you—the reader. They have helped re-shape my life and positioned me so I can inspire, illuminate—but not impose.

The word of God and the promises He made to His children are absolute. Everything else is secondary in nature.

God has always proven to be an integral part of my life's experiences. I knew that no matter what happened, I would always be with Him.

In spite of your adversity, enjoy the life God has given you, no matter what it is.

– Sheila Anthony-Shaw

Courting Sheila:
by Bryan Shaw

My name is Bryan Shaw and I am the very-proud husband of Sheila Anthony-Shaw.

The first memories of being with Sheila are taking her to a doctor appointment in Fremont.

Dozens of exchanged of emails and phone calls would take place before I was in the boyfriend classification. We did not meet face-to-face until three weeks had passed.

When we did date, there was no kissing on the first date, the second date the third date, and dates after that. I believe it was our fifth date that we actually kissed.

Sheila was adhering to a bible-based, teaching she heard. She mentioned a lady whom she greatly admired, but I had never heard of.

Her name is Juanita Bynum.

Okay, I thought. *I am willing to learn something new and see where this leads to.*

Our first date was at Starbucks. After hours of conversation, we decided to have lunch at the *Olive Garden Restaurant.*

I thought she was funny, interesting, and certainly bright.

However, she had not been feeling well, had little energy and was unstable on her feet. I made a point to walk with her whenever we went somewhere.

I was there to see Sheila suddenly lose her equilibrium and strength. One time, while outside of her doctor's office in Fremont, Sheila stumbled and fell. I had never seen anything like that.

She just toppled face-first onto the concrete sidewalk. There was no attempt to catch herself, buckle her knees, or extend her hands to lessen the fall. She just took a header.

Bam!

I was caught off guard and totally surprised that I could not react in time to stop her fall. One minute we were walking out to my car, and the next minute her forehead is hitting the concrete.

I rushed to examine her. There was no blood, but there certainly was evidence of a scrape. She also had a goose-egg sized knot on her forehead and a cracked tooth on the left side of her mouth.

Oddly enough, she always fell to the left. I have since learned to only walk on that side of her wherever we go.

I now know my place after seventeen years together. There were times that I have caught her and called it a success.

Other times, not so good. It was not for the lack of trying, either.

After an icepack for the goose egg and $1,760 for a root canal, I guess I was more taken aback by what she was facing than I was intrigued by her charm, personality, and good looks.

She did pay me back the entire amount when she received a disability settlement. I wasn't really worrying about the money, per se, but rather how she was going to cope going forward.

How can I help her, much less give her a hope for the future in a relationship?

Sheila is my third wife, and the second African American woman that I married.

When my first marriage ended in divorce, I felt like such a failure.

My second marriage ("Hope springs eternal in the breasts of men") was good but ended in death. In some ways I saw that God's healing of the failure of my first marriage and divorce.

God has a funny way of healing.

The scars of my second wife's death run to the core of my very being. They have not been easily forgotten or mended.

I feel like the grief response is constantly there. It lurks in the shadows of my mind, just beyond my own line of sight. The triggers are there-but hidden.

I never know when a grief response will start; nor do I know what the actual triggers for the pain are. That makes it difficult to avoid them.

It's like walking through a field planted with hidden land mines and your metal detector batteries don't work anymore. I am grateful to God that the devastating blows are more and more infrequent.

As Sheila and I talked, I listened to understand what

was going on with her body. I'm an accountant but I've always been an analytical person.

I love history, but not so much as to know what actually went on in the past. I love it because I am curious to why people made the choices they did. Wasn't there some other way to create Yugoslavia from Austria-Hungary's South Slav provinces than killing the Archduke Franz Ferdinand and his bride Sophie?

As I get crankier in my older age I can see why hopelessness and desperation force people to take extreme actions.

But I digress.

Surely, it was possible to find better doctors who would understand her condition and predicament. There had to be someone who was competent enough to help her restore her life.

I wasn't really concerned about her long-term condition. I mean, come on, we live less than an hour's drive from Stanford Medical where they turn out doctors who are not only MDs but PhDs, too.

I refer to these individuals as doctor-doctors.

My late wife was treated by docs at Stanford. The level of care was really good in the teaching hospital. I just didn't count on the emotional toll of getting Sheila into Stanford.

I had no clue it would be such a grief response trigger for me to make that drive to Stanford.

I knew the route well and had driven it countless times. It was going to be easy to get Sheila the help she needed and then we could move on to realizing our dreams and hopes together.

Those were my actual thoughts. In reality, things were quite different.

Here's what I mean by that.

I don't believe we control our thoughts and memories. They come and go like the wind blows the clouds in our skies. To pretend otherwise, is foolish to me.

We discussed children, careers, travel and relatives. Sheila has been very successful in her past vocation and travels. There was no reason to doubt she would not be successful again.

I had been a vice-president of finance for a large multinational high-tech company. We could have a wonderful life of long walks on the beaches of Santa Cruz, and international destinations that I had visited, but had not taken my wife.

I wanted to do something other than just exist with each other.

Sheila is both fun—*and funny*—to be around.

She's amazing. Even when she was in lots of pain, she had a lively mind and great sense of humor. Best of all, she viewed the world through different lenses.

While sitting in a wheelchair, she rattled-off a kind-humor, comedy routine for six minutes about crippled people in the world.

Then, she joked about how no one should ever stand in the vicinity of any pharmacy when meds were not available. She said it's a dangerous place to be when a hurting person is mobile and motivated.

I used comedy to cope, too. I thought it was important to help Sheila keep it together.

Sheila wondered if she would ever find a doctor who understood her condition. After all the blood work, scans and various tests, she was always described as perfectly healthy.

"Healthy as a horse!" I would say that quite often after looking at the lab results.

Thank God there is something called a "Babinski response." It's a reflex that indicates 'abnormal' when there is an autonomic issue in the brain and spine. As such, you can't fake a Babinski.

The doctor's eyebrows would always jump up just like my wife's foot would when they ran the test.

It appeared that they suspected they had another hypochondriac on their hands.

However, Sheila would show them in irrefutable fashion there was something seriously wrong with her perfectly healthy, non-functioning body.

We even had doctors who opted not to get too close to Sheila. They assumed that the unknown disease she had was communicable.

Such nonsense!

I sat there and I would gleefully point out something was wrong. I informed each doctor who feared being contaminated that Sheila did not have a communicable disease.

I let them know that I haven't suffered any ill effects and we regularly shared bodily fluids as husband and wife.

Those logic points did not always go down well with fearful men.

One doctor literally stood in the doorway to the

examining room. He made it very clear that not only was he not the right person to see her, he was unsure of the best treatment for her.

In total, Sheila saw seven neurologists.

We stopped counting doctors after seeing fifty-five different doctors.

When I worked on our tax returns, there were years where we averaged more than $12,000 a year of cash which was spent on medical treatment and medicines.

She weathered the treatments, pokes, indignities and pain with great determination and hope—for the most part, anyway.

There were times when she said, *"no more!"*

As in-no more medical appointments; no more weird medicines, and no more failed treatment plans. Then, four weeks would go by and we were off to see yet another doctor.

Collectively, hundreds of hours were spent researching her symptoms and resources. I recall the day we discovered an alternative medicine school in Santa Cruz, California. There, Sheila tried cupping, acupuncture and Rolfing massages.

I'll never forget the elixir from Costa Rica she tried

exactly one time. It had to be mixed with milk in order for Sheila—or anyone for that matter—to get it down.

That elixir smelled so badly, it made Sheila gagged. We became good at being creative and generating innovative solutions for the mission of getting better.

I came up with the idea of getting my swimming goggles and a nose clip from my truck. We believed that the strategy would help as she drank the concoction down.

It did.

That stuff had a stench that even turned my stomach. It smelled like soured and decaying buttermilk. To think we paid good money for that concoction, and Sheila actually swallowed it.

Ugh.

I'm still shaking my head in disbelief right now as I recall the moment that she drank it.

Among the other alternative treatments she received were recently rediscovered, deep muscle injections of concoctions from the 1950s.

I often use the word, "we" when describing what Sheila went through. That's because seeing my wife subjected to all of this created no real, emotional separation.

Clearly, I was going through it, too.

Sheila was being robbed of her quality of life. It was extremely disappointing. We were desperate to do almost anything if it meant that she would get better.

I was furious.

I knew exactly who it was that was trying to rob, kill, and destroy the abundant life my wife desired to live.

As believers of Jesus Christ and His teachings, we both knew that the enemy of her soul was fighting to keep her down and discouraged. The enemy of her soul was constantly showing his hand, so I prepared myself to step up my warrior response.

I am an accountant by profession. However, unlike most accountants, I do not have a gentle demeanor. Until I was in junior high school, I averaged about a fight a week.

Growing up as a youth in and around Lubbock, Texas, boys and men settled disputes of dishonor and disrespect with their fists. Today, I have several white scars on the back of my hands that are the results of the fights I had.

I declared war on the enemy of my wife's soul. I was

not going to let this go. Nevertheless, I knew that using my fists was uncalled for. This is not that kind of battle. Instead, I went into full warrior mode in prayer.

I walked our house with my Bible open reading scriptures and yelling my prayers for Satan to get out. He had no authority over my family and no place in our house.

I reminded him regularly as to his ultimate fate at the hands of Jesus. I praised Jesus in a very loud fashion.

I'm glad our neighbors didn't live nearby. The homes where we lived at the time were separated by forty yards or more.

I am not quiet when I'm furious and in warrior mode. Even as I write at this moment, my eyes are full of tears of rage and I'm trembling.

As I remember these struggles, I am in warrior-mode. The enemy of my wife's soul *cannot* have her!

We are called to be people of action and so we must step in, even when uncertain. There is a movie that has generated several quotes that we regularly use.

We share them as part of gifts, and unexpected times and when searching hearts for people who are hurting and have no one to stand for them. There is a treasured willingness to venture forth on behalf of the powerless.

It was our kind of movie.

Drug use has never been a factor in my life. I've never used illegal drugs. I have a family history of alcoholism so drinking alcohol for me has not been a priority.

I mention this because it appeared that some of the meds that Sheila were prescribed were very addictive.

One of the neurologists prescribed a medicine that she had a really bad reaction to. She could not sit still.

The second day she took it, it was taking over her life. She stopped taking it after that and tried lots of strategies to get it flushed out of her system.

She drank liters or water and walked throughout the house to exercise and sweat it out of her system. Of course, she could not walk unassisted. We walked together from 10:35 one evening until 6:55 the next morning.

We walked into the closets, around the kitchen island, through each bedroom and around the dining room table. We could not stop moving.

That drug was terrible! And to think, it was prescribed to help her. Instead the reaction was a nightmare. We hoped she had a disease that cannot be named or understood, licked. It had presented itself as the enemy of her soul.

How do you fight against something you cannot see? What was causing this to happen? What must we do next?

Those are a few questions Sheila and I discussed.

There were times early in Sheila's illness that I was incredibly frightened. For example, Sheila was sitting on our couch and I in the rocker when suddenly she gasped. Her back thrust forcefully into the couch and she turned forcefully straight.

Her pelvis pressed up and aligned with her back and stomach and her legs extended. I didn't know it then, but she was having a seizure. There was no warning.

"I can't breathe," she gasped.

Sheila's floating ribs were preventing her lungs from fully expanding. What do I do, first?

Do I run for a washcloth to wipe her face? Rub her shoulders to ease my feelings of clumsiness and inadequacy? Rub her ribcage and try to pull the floating ribs out to allow her to expand her lungs and catch some air?

What lasted about thirty seconds felt like minutes.

Lord, help *now.*

That was my prayer straight from the heart of panic.

It worked.

I'm crying right now as I relive this in my memories. It is still very real to my own soul.

Prayer was the only way I could cope in such a hopeless situation. I felt powerless and lost.

I went to the floor. Knee-top prayers are effective prayers. The pain in my knees diverted my mind from the pain in my soul.

We became, "God watchers." We were looking and expecting to see the grace of God to appear in our lives.

We were not disappointed, either. God *did* show up. It was not as we expected; but He revealed Himself powerful in many ways.

The enemy of my wife's soul was not going to have her without a fight. She was mine and not his. Most importantly, she was the daughter of the King of Kings.

I reminded the enemy of that fact many times. He was going to have to get her out of God's powerful right hand in order to have her.

We needed to cling to each other and to our God. We said we would never give up hope, and we didn't.

Sheila Is the One!

By Bryan Shaw

S heila knew that I was going to marry her before I knew I was going to marry her. As we continued to date and talk, I grew more and more interested in her.

I participated in Bible Study Fellowship for fourteen years. The past six-years I served as a Teaching Leader. My responsibility is to train the leaders and teach the class. At the time, I was a very mature Christian at that stage in my life,

I had come to God as a freshman in college at The University of Texas in Austin through the ministries of the Navigators. They were dedicated to God and taught me a strong foundation in a relationship with God.

I was praying to God regularly about the kind of woman I sought as a wife. I didn't want a girlfriend. I wanted a wife. And I had certain criteria I was seeking in my conversations with God.

As I talked with Sheila about God I listened to her testimony and understanding of who God was in her life. Her love for God was very strong and I was not prepared for one thing she did early on.

Sheila challenged my holiness.

I felt like I was a very mature Christian with a strong love for God. I don't know why that was my response in my spirit.

I sat there stunned, like I had been punched in the chest.

When I thought it through, I realized that she was right. I had slacked off in the closeness with God. It was too casual and lazy. I was neglecting Him as I moved through my days.

My response to her challenge involved increasing the amount of time I was spending with God. This included my personal study, worship, and prayer. I got serious again about God. It wasn't anything she could see.

My feelings for her and her well-being were growing. Neither one of us wanted to be a boyfriend or girlfriend to anyone. I wanted a wife; and she wanted a husband.

As we continued to date, Sheila's financial situation grew bleak. She had to resign from her job because of her disability. Her disability settlement still had not been processed. That meant she had to exhaust her savings and could no longer afford the rent for her apartment.

We agreed that she could live in my house, but not as my wife. She had her own room and key to come and go as she pleased. She could use the kitchen as needed and was allowed access to the rest of the house except the master bedroom.

I was not going to ask Sheila to marry me until I had a clear answer to prayer. I had been praying for a wife before I met Sheila. It was time for me to venture back into life so, I began dating.

Sheila and I kept our distance physically. I didn't like it. I wanted her.

However, it did provide a very serious motivation factor to my prayer life.

I had asked God for three things in a wife:

- She must be a Godly woman.

- She had to have a heart big enough to love another woman's child

- She had to have a wicked sense of humor

Sheila's unknown health situation was troubling to me. Still, I prayed regularly about us moving forward.

However, I refused to discuss marriage with her until I got an answer from God.

Most of the time I don't receive a clear answer from God when I pray; but there are exceptions.

When I get really serious, pray repeatedly, and explain my concerns, I hear His voice just as someone was speaking to me.

There is a clarity and preciseness to his tone and manner of speaking. He does not mince words. I have learned to recognize His voice although I have only heard Him speak a few times.

Not once have I ever felt condemned or judged by Him even when I have deserved a rebuke.

At about 1:45 a.m. on a Sunday morning in the month of January, 2002, I got out of bed to use the restroom. When I returned back to my bed, I sought God's direction and clarity in a decision.

"Should I ask Sheila to marry me? Is she the one I should ask?" I inquired.

I got a clear question in response. It's wasn't what I wanted to hear.

"What have you been asking for?"

I went through my conditions for a wife:

- She must be a Godly woman.

- She had to have a heart big enough to love another woman's child

- She had to have a wicked sense of humor

"But, what about her health?" I asked.

God responded: "You have not asked for that."

I was stunned.

He was right! I had not asked about that previously in my criteria for a wife.

It was very clear to me in my spirit that He had given me exactly what I had asked for and to move ahead.

I respectfully responded, "Okay."

Then, I got up and knocked on Sheila's bedroom door. After entering, I knelt by her and asked her to marry me.

It was not two o'clock in the morning. I proposed to her with neither an engagement ring, nor romantic setting.

When I receive clarity from God I move into action. I always have. I wear size fourteen boots and when I jump into something at God's guidance, I jump in with both feet.

We were married on March 23, 2002.

After ninety-seven days of marriage, Sheila's health spiraled down for the next ten years.

She went from walking with a cane occasionally, to not being able to walk at all. There was a wheelchair in our garage and she began to use that.

Sheila is a fighter by nature and I'm stubborn. The combination made it easier to hold onto each other throughout the entire process of ill-health.

Also, as Christians, our hopes are rooted in God's strength and faithfulness. We're not going to separate from God for any reason.

I suppose I'm a warrior at heart. I saw this much like a battle to be won. I just could not find the right solution to restore the abundant life my wife was promised by God.

The Wright One by

Bryan Shaw

D r. David Craig Wright is a Godsend.

Sheila was referred to him by her massage therapist. At the time, she was in so much pain she could barely be touched—much less benefit from a deep-tissue massage.

The therapist had a special needs son and Dr. Wright had helped him greatly. She urged Sheila to try one more doctor. If Dr. Wright could not help, no one could. That's what she believed.

He is an infectious diseases specialist who retired from the east coast to practice in Monterey, California. A true lover of jazz, he moved his family to the region because Monterey was famous for its jazz festival.

To the point, there are six chairs for patients, and two grand pianos which grace his office waiting room. It's hard not to respect a man who has his priorities right.

After retiring, Dr. Wright saw many hurting people in California. They were not being treated properly—medically speaking. This inspired him to reopen his clinic.

As a longstanding doctor at Walter Reed Hospital in Maryland, he specialized in exotic poisons generated from jelly fish stings, spiders, scorpions, snakes, and other lovely creatures.

Impressively, Dr. David Craig Wright has his name on about fifteen patents. This guy loves medicine and learning about new medicine.

He opened the first AIDS clinic in the America; and was the first American government doctor to officially visit the Peoples' Republic of China medical system.

Dr. Wright shared that he has treated C.I.A. agents but has never been in their employ.

I told him that I thought he was a C.I.A. doctor because he knows such weird stuff about poisons and such.

He laughed and said he wasn't.

On November 30, 2012, Sheila and I saw Dr. Wright for the first time. She brought a box of her medical records with her which she had accumulated over several years.

In total, it was three pages short of a ream of paper. A ream is five hundred pages.

Dr. Wright met with us for about ninety minutes. In that time, he gave her a full examination from the bottom of her soles, to the top of her head.

He actually felt and even examined her scalp.

I'm not sure what he was looking for, but he was completely thorough.

When he finished, he scheduled her next appointment during the first week of January, 2013. And gave her a lab slip and sent her off to the local, Quest Laboratories for blood work.

We would not know the results until we saw Dr. Wright five weeks, later.

During the doctor visits with Dr. Wright over the years, Sheila and I found nothing unusual about any of them except the length of time he spent with her.

I recall the times when he would stop speaking and seemingly, begin to think about possibilities. He'd close his eyes, lean back in his chair, and rub his round belly in a light-mannered circle.

Then he'd suddenly launch into another series of questions for us to answer.

It was a hard, five weeks to wait for results.

The day of Sheila's appointment, Dr. Wright did not waste any time. After greeting us both, he looked at Sheila.

"I know more about what is going on with your body now," he stated matter-of-factly.

He continued. "I know what is wrong with you. I know how to treat you, and I know how to get the treatment paid for. Are you ready to hear?"

We sat in his office with stunned looks on our faces.

We literally were struck dumb by what he said. In all of the eleven years I had known Sheila, I had never had a doctor say that to either of us.

Dr. Wright laughed at our reactions. Sheila composed herself enough to reply, "Yes, please!"

My wife is always very respectful to the doctors; I, less so.

The doctor said that my wife had tick-borne, relapsing fever and WPA6 Something.

The WPA6 Something disease was so rare it didn't even have a name. We were familiar with Lyme disease and Rocky Mountain spotted fever. Both are commonly caught from hard-shell deer ticks.

However, what Sheila had was commonly transmitted by soft-shelled ticks and are typically found on bats, squirrels, and rats. The soft-shelled tick bites, and then drops off. Most of the time, people are unaware that they have been in contact with a tick.

The majority of California doctors only tested Sheila for Lyme disease. Apparently, they were not familiar with any of the other types of tick-borne pathogens. They're not common diseases thought to plague Californians.

Interesting enough, a recent tick survey was performed at Stevens Creek County Park in Santa Clara County. The results plainly showed a multitude of ticks infested with a variety of tick-borne diseases.

At the time of this writing, there are more than twelve types of diseases you can catch from ticks.

Dr. Wright went on and on about Barbeosis and the other types of weird tick diseases she didn't have.

This was unexpected. Sheila listened in shock.

Indeed, she had already planned some shopping therapy in Monterey after visiting with Dr. Wright. She figured there wouldn't be any good news to learn from this new doctor.

Before seeing Dr. Wright that day, the two of us had

set in our minds to go to the *Forever 21* store in Monterey after Sheila's appointment. She could always count on finding a pair of earrings or shoes at *Forever 21*. It made her feel better about herself.

The doctor wanted to immediately begin administering her treatment. It consisted of forty-two consecutive days of antibiotics administered through an IV.

I'm good at math. forty-two days is six weeks.

That's a lot of antibiotics!

At the end of treatment from forty-two straight days of IVs, she had another blood test that showed very low levels of infection.

I couldn't help but notice that Dr. Wright did not look the least concerned that the infection was still present. But he knew something that I didn't.

My eyebrows raised a little.

"We're not done yet?" I asked.

Dr. Wright looked at me and smiled before saying, "Let's wait and see what happens."

Four months after beginning IV treatments, Sheila's blood test result revealed that not only was she completely free of the tick-borne relapsing fever infection, but the WPA6 Something infection was in remission.

We were thrilled. *Praise God!*

After seven years, Sheila is still is a patient of Dr. Wright, today. He monitors her progress and healing.

She has gone from a wheelchair, to walker to a four-prong cane to a cane.

Most days the cane stays in one corner of the kitchen and Sheila walks throughout our house without assistance.

When she leaves the house for the day, she always takes the cane for stability and comfort purposes.

I think her mind has not caught up with her body's healing yet.

Dr. Wright was indeed sent to us by God. And, at just the right time.

In 2017, the Centers for Disease Control and Prevention (CDC) stopped providing assays to blood labs.

The assays are necessary to run the types of tests Dr. Wright performed at Quest Laboratories.

Without them, the tests cannot absolutely confirm

the presence of tick-borne relapsing fever.

Dr. Wright continues to fight with the CDC on this decision. He is seeking alternative solutions to develop and use assays to diagnose people with tick diseases.

At the time of this writing, he is working with some wealthy donors to form a medical school and related lab in Fresno County. The goal is to develop the types of blood assays the CDC has discontinued.

Dr. Wright is a Godsend.

If my wife had not seen him when she did, she would still not have been conclusively diagnosed.

As long as there is no absolute diagnosis, there is no payment of the treatment plan. It's a clever way to avoid payments by the disability branch of Social Security.

And, if the doctor can't test for the disease, then it can't be diagnosed. There is no payment for treatments for "suspected conditions." This is the world we currently live in; but God's timing is perfect.

David Craig Wright, MD

Board Certified in Internal Medicine and Infectious Disease, Dr. David Craig Wright holds fifteen patents and is a graduate of the College of Arts and Sciences and the Medical School at the University of Virginia in Charlottesville, VA.

He completed his internship at Columbia Presbyterian/Harlem Hospital in New York and his residency in Internal Medicine and Infectious Disease and Tropical Medicine training at Walter Reed Army Medical Center in Washington, D.C.

In 2009, Dr. David Craig Wright came out of retirement after over 30 years of experience seeing patients and working in the biopharmaceutical industry to open a private practice in Carmel, California.

Dr. Wright moved his practice to Monterey, CA and opened up the infusion center in 2010. There, an infectious disease expert is onsite 365 days per year, 7 a.m. to 7 p.m.

The Center's rates are at least 50 percent lower than hospitals. The lowest cost provider for intravenous antibiotic therapy, Dr. Wright's Infusion Center also administers anti-infectives, immunoglobulins, and intravenous reclast for osteoporosis, as well as mercury-free, unit dose, Influenza vaccines.

For more information, please call the Center at (831) 717 4444 or visit 80 Garden Court Road, Suite 102, Monterey, CA.

Acknowledgements

Writing my memoir was more challenging than I imagined. However, it's been a rewarding experience that I wouldn't trade for anything.

I am truly grateful to all who have made this memoir possible.

First and foremost, I give honor and glory to God who has been with me before I entered this world as we know it. Thank you for every step of this spectacular journey. I fully expect to have many more steps in the future.

Thank you, Dr. David C. Wright. You have made my life—and the lives of innumerable others—immeasurably better.

Were it not for your intervention, God knows that I would not be writing this today. Thank you for the life-transforming infusion antibiotic, immunotherapy, and IV therapy. And thank you for the invaluable education.

I also thank you for your kind and humorous disposition. You made the process comfortable.

I find it absolutely fascinating that what started as a thought manifested into a vision shared with many. It's been a joy to see how it grew and magnified in my eyes as well as in the eyes of others.

Thank you, Bryan Shaw. You provided invaluable tools and ideas which encouraged me to manifest the vision.

Husband, you have done more than that: you stuck by me through the most trying times a marriage could ever experience. Your countless contributions to my life and others do not go unnoticed. You, Bryan Shaw, are my Godsend.

Mia Thompson Gordon. Niece, have you any idea how grateful I am for you and your life-altering ideas? Where would I be had I not acted upon *most* of them?

For one thing, I probably wouldn't be enjoying the bay area with you and loving your sister and family.

Thank you for recommending Fran Briggs as my literary representative, publicist, and content editor. You were right; she is everything you said, and more. I love and appreciate you!

Fran Briggs. My energy resonated with you during

our first conversation. Thank you for your patience, brilliance, and vision. It has been exciting and fulfilling journey learning about the literary process.

When I momentarily became overwhelmed, your "No worries; all is well," quickly help me put things back into perspective.

I thank God for gifting you with a multitude of talents. Your editorial assistance, keen insight, and continuous support all helped to bring my story to life.

Whether it's refining my ideas; encouraging me to keep my timelines; or paying alms to me for demonstrating resilience despite all that has come against me, I could count on you for your consistency.

You brought out what I had forgotten what was inside me.

Thank you, Cynthia Johnson; Associate Publishers of www.DiverseSkillsCenter.com, Florida; Jordan Briggs, Arizona; Rebecca; Kori Raishon, New York; and Lyndal Spirit, Colorado; Divonne Jackson, Detroit, Michigan; and Nicole Bradley, IN; Gary Community School Corporation. Your contribution towards the publication of this book is very-much appreciated.

To my siblings: Jesse Anthony; Jean Coward; Anne Anthony; Charles Anthony; and Francis John Coward, respectively. I was honored to present you to the world!

You are my best friends. Thank you for being providers of equal amounts of kindness and bluntness. I am blessed to have you all in my life.

To *Pepsi,* thank you for being the only sponsor for the only event that was offered me during my reign as Miss Fresno County, 1980.

The tree loggers' event was in an extremely remote and sparsely populated area of the Fresno County (California), but you came through as the title sponsor and sponsored my float appearance.

I know that I am not accepting an Oscar award, but it sure does feel like it.

To all the individuals who gave me the opportunity to lead at *Bank of America* and *Cellular One.* You recognized my abilities and aptitude, brought me on as an employee, and then equipped me to rise through the ranks. For that, I am grateful.

Finally, to all those who have been a part of me getting here: My congregations, teachers, women's fellowship group, professors, coaches, doctors, therapists, attorneys, neighbors, and friends—especially all of you who do not see your name on this page, thank you for your unconditional love and unrelenting support.

Partners of Prestige

It's been said that it's always bittersweet when an author finishes a book, that's because of the countless individuals who supported the writer throughout the process.

However, there is something that I can take comfort in, and express the utmost appreciation for: my Partners of Prestige.

I am extremely grateful to the following sponsors, patrons, and friends who are making my post activities, possible.

They have been both enthusiastic supporters, and great sources for encouragement, as well.

I can't imagine where I'd be without them. Because of their generous support, my team and I are able to present a world-class, book launch, tour, and community outreach.

With Gratitude,

Sheila Anthony-Shaw

Dr. David Craig Wright

Atiya and Erik Smith

Renee and Don Polk

Francis and Maureen Coward

Alan Chinn & Spouse

Kent and Lillie Turner

Bill and Kim Douglas

Dave and Emmylou Cerf

Joy and Ed Washington

Kristin and Rick Mandia

Elaine Andersen & Spouse

Christianne Yates (PMI Realtor) - Christiansen's

Prisca and Bryant Walton

Pastor Hurmon Hamilton & Dr. Rhonda Hamilton

Pastor Jennifer Chapman

Johan de Quant

About Sheila Anthony-Shaw

Sheila Anthony (Shaw) was born in Houston, Texas. As a twenty-one-year-old in 1980, Sheila made history when she became the first African American to win the Miss Fresno County beauty pageant in the contest's 35-year history. She attended Fresno State University, where she majored in Radio/TV Broadcasting with a double minor in English and Journalism. After winning the Miss Fresno County title, Sheila went on to enjoy successful management careers with Bank of America and Cellular One, respectively. Today, she speaks and writes with the aim of helping others enjoy happier and healthier lives.

Made in the USA
San Bernardino, CA
04 July 2019